THE RESPONSIBLE
SERVING OF
ALCOHOLIC
BEVERAGES:

A COMPLETE STAFF TRAINING COURSE FOR BARS, RESTAURANTS, AND CATERERS

By Beth Dugan

THE RESPONSIBLE SERVING OF ALCOHOLIC BEVERAGES: A COMPLETE STAFF TRAINING COURSE FOR BARS, RESTAURANTS, AND CATERERS

Copyright © 2006 by Atlantic Publishing Group, Inc.

1210 SW 23rd Place • Ocala, Florida 34474 • 800-814-1132 • 352-622-5836–Fax

Web site: www.atlantic-pub.com • E-mail sales@atlantic-pub.com

SAN Number :268-1250

ISBN-13: 978-0-910627-63-4   ISBN-10: 0-910627-63-0

Library of Congress Cataloging-in-Publication Data

Dugan, Beth.

The responsible serving of alcoholic beverages : a complete staff training course for bars, restaurants, and caterers / Beth Dugan.

p. cm.

Includes index.

ISBN-13: 978-0-910627-63-4 (alk. paper)

1. Bars (Drinking establishments) 2. Drinking of alcoholic beverages. 3. Hospitality industry--Management. I. Title.

TX950.7.D82 2006

647.95'068--dc22

2005032546

Printed in the United States

ART DIRECTION, FRONT COVER & INTERIOR DESIGN: Meg Buchner • megadesn@mchsi.com

BOOK PRODUCTION DESIGN: Studio 6 Sense • info@6sense.net • www.6sense.net

TABLE OF CONTENTS

SECTION I
INTRODUCTION TO RESPONSIBLE BEVERAGE SERVICE

Introduction

CHAPTER 1: WHAT IS ALCOHOL?

CHAPTER 2: SERVING ALCOHOL AND THE LAW

SECTION II MANAGEMENT RESPONSIBILITIES WHEN SERVING ALCOHOL

CHAPTER 3: FIND YOUR TARGET CUSTOMERS

CHAPTER 4: TYPES OF OPERATIONS AND RESPONSIBLE BEVERAGE SERVICE

CHAPTER 5: TYPES OF CUSTOMERS AND RESPONSIBLE BEVERAGE SERVICE

CHAPTER 6: YOUR ESTABLISHMENT AND RESPONSIBLE ALCOHOL SERVICE

CHAPTER 7: YOUR OFFERINGS AND RESPONSIBLE BEVERAGE SERVICE

CHAPTER 8: SERVING POLICIES AND RESPONSIBLE BEVERAGE SERVICE

CHAPTER 9: EMPLOYEES AND RESPONSIBLE BEVERAGE SERVICE

CHAPTER 10: WHEN BAD THINGS HAPPEN TO GOOD BARS

SECTION III   THE TRAINING PROGRAM

CHAPTER 11: CUSTOMIZING YOUR PLAN FOR YOUR ESTABLISHMENT

MODULE 1: LEGAL ISSUES SURROUNDING SERVING ALCOHOL

LEGAL ISSUES: TRAINING MODULE

MODULE 2: ALCOHOL AND THE BODY

ALCOHOL AND THE BODY: TRAINING MODULE

MODULE 3: GREEN-YELLOW-RED SYSTEM AND ASSESSING AND SERVING CUSTOMERS

GREEN-YELLOW-RED SYSTEM AND STRATEGIES FOR THEIR USE

MODULE 4: REFRESHER COURSES

REFRESHER COURSE

APPENDIX

GLOSSARY

REFERENCES

SECTION ONE

INTRODUCTION TO RESPONSIBLE BEVERAGE SERVICE

INTRODUCTION

T*he Reponsible Serving of Alcoholic Beverages* is designed to help bar owners and managers make necessary changes, and train their employees in order to mitigate legal risks when serving alcohol. This book includes sections on policy changes as well as a bar training program. Managers can use the companion CD, and print out those parts most applicable to their operation.

WHY READ THIS BOOK?

Running a bar today can be very difficult. Even something as simple as getting a liquor license, so that your customers can have a beer with their pizza, is complicated by the issues surrounding alcohol. Some of our customers, and some bar owners, have not always had the public in mind when selling and drinking alcohol, causing serious social issues. As a seller of alcohol, you need to understand that the climate is changing, increasing your burden of ensuring that everyone who drinks in your establishment leaves without causing harm.

Attitudes relating to serving alcohol have become more restrictive during the last few years. Dram shop laws are part of this process, but it also includes signage requirements, age of server policies, advertising restrictions, and, most recently, the lowering of blood alcohol concentration (BAC) levels. As an owner or manager, in some localities you could face citations for doing something as simple as using pitchers. This book tries to show examples of beverage service and suggests how you can mitigate risks while serving liquor.

This book is based on research from accepted medical, legal, and scholarly sources concerning bar management and serving alcohol. It is based on the premise that a bar owner has a responsibility toward the general public, and that drinkers of legal age are adults. This book will help you to run a customer-friendly yet legally responsible bar.

So what is a customer-friendly yet legally responsible bar? It is a bar where customers relax, have a drink or two, maybe something to eat, and perhaps listen to music. People have their own ideas of what makes a good bar, and their ideal Monday-night bar may be very different from their ideal Saturday-night bar. What you, the owner, are aiming at is a place where the customer has fun and consumes alcohol in a reasonable manner. By creating an atmosphere where activities, good conversation, or great music are present, customers can come to enjoy themselves.

But, some of you are thinking, *If alcohol is the main part of my revenue, how can I survive if customers don't drink until drunk?* You can be profitable by increasing check averages with higher-priced drinks, food, or other items, by creating

amusements that customers will spend money on, and by
having staff who monitor consumption and take action when
needed. Looking long and hard at your policies and controls
means that you will soon find that you may be able to make
more of a profit with responsible service, and have fewer
hassles from intoxicated patrons.

Dealing with inebriated guests is no fun. No one likes to
cut someone off or have to argue with a drunk who wants
to drive home. Next to cleaning a fryer, it is probably one of
the worst jobs in the industry. It is better not to have your
customers get into that situation rather than to have to deal
with the aftermath. This book will help you to prevent such
problems.

WHO SHOULD READ THIS BOOK?

This book is for managers and owners: the people in a
bar who can make and influence changes within their
operation. It gives an overview of how to create a legally safe
environment, while remaining customer friendly. The goal
of this book is to help bar owners mitigate their legal risks
without sacrificing sales or profitability.

The third part of the book contains a general training
program designed for managers to train serving personnel
such as waiters and bartenders. The program will need
modification depending upon your locality and your local
laws concerning alcoholic beverage training programs.
However, because most of the work is done, only a few hours
of preparation are needed in order to complete the training

program and begin scheduling classes.

HOW TO USE THIS BOOK

To start, finish reading this section and then move on to Section II. Find your state's laws in the Appendix and use them for reference within Section II's chapters. This section deals with the areas that a bar manager can control and fix to make their bar legally safer. At the end of each chapter in that section you will find space to note where you need to make changes or highlight suggestions for your staff. After analyzing risky areas, you can make changes to your bar's environment. Next, using the information at the end of the chapters, you can begin to modify the training program located in Section III to make it unique to your operation.

WHAT OTHER TOPICS DOES THIS BOOK COVER?

Since this book is primarily about the responsible service of alcohol, it only covers that topic. If you're looking for information on general bar management, check out our titles *Professional Bar and Beverage Manager's Handbook: How to Open and Operate a Financially Successful Bar, Tavern and Nightclub* or *How to Manage a Successful Bar,* both available from Atlantic Publishing. These two books cover the management, marketing, and financial information needed to run a bar. Instant Bartender CD, also from Atlantic Publishing, covers drink recipes. Make sure that you check out the collection of posters on Alcohol Awareness that are available at the Atlantic Publishing Web site, **www.atlantic-pub.com**. For cost-cutting ideas on managing your bar, check out *The Food Service Manager's Guide to Creative Cost Cutting and Cost Control: Over 2,001 Innovative and Simple Ways to Save Thousands by Reducing Expenses.*

ALCOHOL AWARENESS POSTER: Symptoms of Intoxication

Posters are printed in full color and laminated to reduce wear and tear. It measures 11" x 17". Available from Atlantic Publishing, Item # SIO-PS, $9.95. To order, call 1-800-814-1132 or visit www.atlantic-pub.com.

CHAPTER

1

WHAT IS ALCOHOL?

This section explains what alcohol is and how it affects people. Its history, chemical composition, and medical effects are discussed.

WHAT IS ALCOHOL?

A natural substance, alcohol is a complex chemical compound created in several ways. Of the four general types, ethanol, made from plant material, is the only form consumable by humans. Since a weak form of beer can be a byproduct of bread, alcohol has been around for some time, as shown by archeological evidence.

Most alcohol is categorized as fermented or distilled. To make fermented alcohol, the process begins with mashing and heating plant material, after which sugar and yeast are added and alcohol is allowed to develop. Grains, such as barley or wheat, ferment to produce a member of the beer family, and grapes produce wine. Fermented products usually top out at 14 percent of alcohol by volume because the chemical relationship between sugar and yeast will not allow them to go much higher. Beer and wine are the most popular types of fermented products, although ciders, meads, and fruit wines also fall into this category.

Distilled beverages are made from a fermented base. Plant material, such as corn, is fermented and distilled by adding water to the base and heating it under pressure. The steam is captured by a series of tubes and, when cooled, almost pure alcohol is left behind, picking up the taste of the original mash. Alcohol can be further distilled and refined increasing the volume of alcohol compared to water each time it occurs. Distilled beverages range from 15 percent alcohol to almost 100 percent alcohol by volume. Because of this, distilled beverages pack more of a punch than fermented ones. Distilled beverages are normally aged after production, as their taste can be quite harsh. All spirits, such as vodkas, gins, rums, whiskeys, and cordials, are distilled beverages.

A third category of beverages exists called blended. Most blends start with a fermented beverage, such as wine, and then the corresponding distillate is added. However, since their alcohol content is close to distilled beverages, you can safely treat them as such.

Alcohol straight out of the bottle may also contain other additives hidden as trade secrets. Usually it contains water, remnants of the original flavor agent, and additional flavors—natural and artificial—to boost its taste. Neon-colored cordials may also contain color additives. Moreover, preservatives such as sulfites may have been added. Additional ingredients or additives are listed on ingredient panels on the back of the bottle, but labeling laws are not consistent across products, and imported items may be exempt. For further information, check with your liquor sales representative especially for common allergens such as sulfites, which customers may inquire about.

HOW DOES ALCOHOL AFFECT THE BODY?

As soon as someone has an alcoholic drink, some of the alcohol enters the bloodstream directly from the mouth. The rest passes to the stomach and small intestine where it's absorbed by passing through the cell walls and into the bloodstream. Alcohol circulates until the liver can break it down. Since the liver can only break down approximately one drink per hour, the remaining alcohol keeps circulating in the bloodstream until the liver can process it. This circulating alcohol (which enters into and interferes with the workings of the body's cells) causes the characteristics of intoxication. Once broken down, alcohol is excreted as urine through the bladder. Within three minutes of drinking, alcohol begins to hit the brain via the bloodstream.

Alcohol and the initial ingredients used in the fermentation process have some health benefits—in small doses. A moderate use of alcohol appears to have a beneficial effect on coronary heart disease acting as a "roto-router" for the arteries. Alcohol may also prevent some types of strokes, but heavy drinking increases the risk of other types. A drink can help customers relax and unwind. Alcohol has some pain relief benefits, although the amount needed for severe pain is close to coma level. Paired with food, wines and beers can elevate the taste of some dishes. Wine has long been used in religious ceremonies cementing its relationship with special landmarks in people's lives.

If a little alcohol is good, then a lot of alcohol can be bad. It appears — especially for women — that alcohol can increase blood pressure. Heavy drinkers and alcoholics are at significant risk of contracting alcoholic hepatitis, or cirrhosis of the liver, and some forms of cancer. Alcohol can also interfere with fetal development and the effectiveness of most popularly prescribed medications.

Alcohol acts on the brain as a depressant, shutting down the higher reasoning centers causing a loss of control and inhibitions. After this, alcohol goes to work on the cerebral cortex and neural base functions: the automatic part of the brain that controls breathing, heart rate, and the digestive tract. Once this section is shut down, the individual is in a coma, near death, and extremely hard to resuscitate.

Alcohol also acts as a diuretic. To process alcohol, the liver pulls water from cells increasing the drinker's thirst. As water depletes, the person's thirst will increase — possibly causing them to drink more alcohol. The diuretic properties of alcohol also interfere with normal bladder control, creating a need to urinate more often and thus further depleting the system of water.

Alcohol causes the blood vessels near the surface of the skin to expand, creating a flush and sense of warmth in the person drinking. Customers at this level perceive the ambient room temperature as being very warm. For those who are heavy drinkers, repeated damage could result in permanent flushing of the skin.

Alcohol also interferes with the body's ability to regulate blood sugar. Because alcohol takes priority over sugar, the liver focuses on breaking down alcohol, allowing excess sugar to circulate within the bloodstream. The sugar overload influences appetite and causes headaches followed by hangovers, as the sugar continues to travel in the bloodstream waiting for the alcohol to leave. Once the alcohol is gone, it takes the now-overworked liver a few more hours to process the sugar before the final side effects of drinking are gone.

WHAT IS BAC?

What is an alcoholic – is it different from being a drunk?

Anyone can get drunk – when you drink too much alcohol and reach a state of intoxication where you are stumbling around, your state is based on how much you drink and how your body handles alcohol. Once your liver processes it out of your system, you are no longer drunk or affected by the alcohol.

Alcoholics, on the other hand, seem to have some sort of "glitch" that causes their bodies to process alcohol differently than other people. Alcohol affects their neural transmitters in such a way that they are dependent upon alcohol to make their neurons work properly. It seems that this "glitch" is genetically preprogrammed, and in some people, the neurons respond to drugs, shopping, overeating, or gambling instead of alcohol.

Alcoholics are physically and emotionally dependent on the bottle to maintain equilibrium and can't go without for their body to function. But alcohol takes a toll on an alcoholic's body over time, causing problems with their liver, brain, heart, and other organs. This will cause problems day in and day out. Since the only treatment method offered to alcoholics at this time is abstinence, a patient needs to be psychologically ready to begin treatment before it will work. Forcing an alcoholic into treatment will cause a temporary cessation of drinking, but, come a crisis, they will be back to where they were before unless they initiate treatment themselves.

Does everyone who has this genetic "glitch" become an alcoholic? It appears that environment also has a role in the process. A child with the "glitch," who grows up seeing their parents take a drink whenever times are tough, may develop alcoholism later. Or they may turn into a drug addict, gambler, or compulsive shopper. Another child with the "glitch," who sees their parents work out problems without resorting to alcohol, may learn important skills that lessen destructive behavior or the need for alcohol.

Can someone without the "glitch" become an alcoholic? Again, the evidence is sketchy on this topic. Certainly, a person can become emotionally dependent upon alcohol, needing the calming influence that its depressive properties bring. However, whether or not a daily drink interferes with the brain to the extent that neural transmitters are damaged is a hotly debated topic in the medical industry. For some alcoholics, identifying the stressor that causes them to drink may go a long way toward helping them get off the bottle and giving them skills for life.

Blood alcohol content (BAC) is the amount of alcohol compared to blood in a person's body at a particular point in time. A BAC of 0.1 means that for every 1,000 drops of blood, one drop of alcohol is present. The only way to measure a person's BAC accurately is with a breathalyzer test or by drawing blood—two methods not usually available in the local watering hole.

Since BAC is dependent upon the amount of blood in a person's body, heavier and taller customers will have a lower BAC than shorter, lighter people after the same number of drinks. Body composition—for example, the difference between an athlete and the same-weight couch potato—also influences blood volume and BAC. Since there is no way of knowing anyone's exact BAC at any given time, most establishments use two different tests to approximate BAC levels.

The first method uses a BAC behavior chart. Comparing a patron's behavior with the chart means that an approximate level can be determined. This method, known as "probable cause" by law officials, shows a type of behavior with an associated BAC level. The chart is based on averages; each person is different and may be affected by alcohol differently each time they drink. On the following pages, some factors that may affect the absorption of alcohol and BAC levels are listed.

BAC LEVELS AND EFFECTS

The following chart gives the external cues that correlate to the approximate BAC level.

BLOOD ALCOHOL CONTENT LEVEL—EFFECTS ON THE PERSON	
.02	The customer feels warm and relaxed.
.04	Individuals are relaxed, soothed, and are talking more freely. Their skin may show some flushing. They may begin to remove outer clothing or complain that the room temperature is "too hot."
.05	The first signs of changes in behavior are observed; for example, lightheartedness, giddiness, and lowered inhibitions. Both restraint and judgment are lowered, coordination may be altered, and moods may swing.
.06	Judgment may become impaired. Reaction time is much slower. Maneuvering and the ability to make decisions are clearly impaired.
.08	Definite impairment of muscle coordination and a slower reaction time; the customer's driving ability may be suspect. Their cheeks and lips are numb. Their hands, arms, and legs may tingle and then feel numb. This is the legally drunk level in some states.
.10	They are clumsy and their speech may become unclear. Their reaction time and muscle control have deteriorated. This is the legally drunk level in the rest of the states, and it is illegal to operate a motor vehicle with this or a greater BAC in all states.

BLOOD ALCOHOL CONTENT LEVEL—EFFECTS ON THE PERSON	
.15	The customer's balance and movement are clearly impaired.
.20	Their motor and emotional control centers are measurably affected. They suffer from slurred speech. Staggering, loss of balance, and double vision can occur.
.30	They have a lack of understanding of what they see or hear. The individual is often confused about their actions. Consciousness may be lost at this level; that, is the individual "passes out."
.40	Usually unconscious; skin clammy.
.45	Respiration slows and can stop altogether.
.50	This level of intoxication can result in coma or death.

Another way to calculate BAC is to use standard drink charts. The charts are based on a person's approximate weight and sex, as men metabolize alcohol at a slower rate than women. The charts include the number of drinks per hour less the amount (.0015 BAC) metabolized by the liver. These charts are approximations as each individual may metabolize alcohol at a slightly different rate. When using the charts, make sure that you look at the correct one: pick the one with the correct number of drinks over the number of hours that the person has been in the bar. A person who consumes five drinks in one hour will be more intoxicated than a person who consumes the same five drinks over the course of five hours. As each hour goes by, their liver metabolizes the alcohol, lessening the amount in their bloodstream. Some standard drink charts are included in this chapter.

Why are there two charts – one for men and the other for women?

It seems that alcohol affects men and women differently for a variety of reasons. Men generally have a higher percentage of water in their bodies, thus diluting alcohol as it hits the bloodstream. Men are also generally larger and more muscular than women of equal weight. Finally, there appears to be a relationship between female sex hormones and how fast the liver metabolizes alcohol.

Men, who have some female hormones (but obviously not as many as women) have a steadier and slower rate of metabolism.

BLOOD ALCOHOL CONTENT CHART—MEN	
1 Drink = 12-oz Beer	1 Drink = 4-oz Table Wine
1 Drink = 1-oz 100 Proof Liquor	1 Drink = 1-oz 80 Proof Liquor

These charts have a one-drink-per-hour elimination factor.

For Men	After 1 Hour of Drinking						
	Weight						
Drinks	120	140	160	180	200	220	240
1	.015	.010	.007	.004	.002	.001	.000
2	.046	.036	.030	.024	.020	.018	.014
3	.077	.062	.053	.044	.038	.035	.029
4	.108	.088	.076	.064	.056	.052	.044
5	.139	.114	.099	.094	.074	.069	.059
6	.170	.140	.122	.104	.092	.086	.074

BLOOD ALCOHOL CONTENT CHART—MEN							
7	.201	.166	.145	.124	.110	.108	.089

For Men	After 2 Hours of Drinking						
	Weight						
Drinks	120	140	160	180	200	220	240
1	.000	.000	.000	.000	.000	.000	.000
2	.030	.020	.014	.008	.004	.002	.000
3	.061	.046	.037	.028	.022	.019	.013
4	.092	.072	.060	.048	.040	.036	.028
5	.123	.098	.083	.068	.058	.053	.043
6	.154	.114	.106	.088	.076	.070	.058
7	.185	.150	.129	.108	.194	.087	.073

For Men	After 3 Housr of Drinking						
	Weight						
Drinks	120	140	160	180	200	220	240
1	.014	.004	.000	.000	.000	.000	.000
2	.045	.030	.021	.012	.006	.003	.000
3	.076	.056	.044	.032	.024	.020	.012
4	.107	.082	.067	.052	.042	.037	.027
5	.138	.108	.090	.072	.060	.054	.052
6	.169	.134	.113	.092	.078	.071	.057
7	.200	.160	.138	.112	.096	.088	.072

FACTORS OWNERS CAN INFLUENCE

While each person reacts differently to alcohol, there are ways in which a bar owner can help to slow down the rate of absorption.

Serve Food

Food will slow down alcohol's passage into the small intestine. Amazingly, the old bar standbys of fried, fatty foods slow down alcohol the most; for example, chicken wings and strips, battered vegetable appetizers, and breaded fried cheese nuggets. Selling appetizers with beer is one way to slow down the absorption rate for a customer. Suggest food whenever someone orders a drink. For late nights after the cook goes home, frozen pizzas and pizza ovens may be a great addition for behind the bar. They also increase sales for the establishment.

Carbonated Drinks

Carbonation, shown by the fizzy bubbles in some drinks, helps to speed alcohol through the stomach and into the small intestine. Bartenders should serve champagne and any soda-based drinks carefully, as they speed up the rate of intoxication.

Amount of Alcohol in the Drink

Different drink families have different amounts of liquor in them. For example, rum and Coke is one alcohol unit mixed with soda. A martini is made of gin and vermouth —two alcohol units plus garnish. Long Island Iced Tea is made by combining several units of alcohol with soda. Every bartender needs to know how to count drinks and how much liquor should go into each glass. Managers need to create recipes and standard measures for each drink that allow accurate counting by servers. If a bartender over-pours or does not follow recipes, the customer may become intoxicated sooner than expected because of extra alcohol in their drink.

BLOOD ALCOHOL CONTENT CHART—WOMEN	
1 Drink = 12-oz Beer	1 Drink = 4-oz Table Wine
1 Drink = 1-oz 100 Proof Liquor	1 Drink = 1-oz 80 Proof Liquor

These charts have a one-drink-per-hour elimination factor.

For Women	After 1 Hour of Drinking							
	Weight							
Drinks	100	120	140	160	180	200	220	240
1	.029	.021	.016	.012	.009	.006	.004	.002
2	.074	.058	.048	.040	.034	.028	.024	.020
3	.119	.095	.080	.068	.059	.050	.044	.038
4	.164	.132	.112	.096	.084	.072	.064	.056
5	.209	.169	.144	.124	.109	.094	.084	.074
6	.253	.206	.176	.152	.134	.116	.104	.092
7	.299	.243	.208	.180	.159	.138	.124	.110

For Women	After 2 Hours of Drinking							
	Weight							
Drinks	100	120	140	160	180	200	220	240
1	.013	.005	.000	.000	.000	.000	.000	.000
2	.058	.042	.032	.024	.018	.012	.008	.004
3	.103	.079	.064	.052	.043	.034	.028	.022
4	.148	.116	.096	.080	.068	.056	.048	.040

For Women	After 2 Hours of Drinking						
5	.193	.153	.128	.108	.093	.078	.068	.058
6	.238	.190	.160	.136	.118	.100	.088	.076
7	.283	.227	.192	.164	.143	.122	.108	.094

For Women	After 3 Hours of Drinking							
	Weight							
Drinks	100	120	140	160	180	200	220	240
2	.042	.026	.016	.008	.002	.000	.000	.000
3	.087	.063	.048	.036	.027	.018	.012	.006
4	.132	.100	.080	.064	.052	.040	.032	.024
5	.177	.137	.112	.092	.077	.062	.052	.042
6	.222	.174	.144	.120	.102	.084	.072	.060
7	.267	.211	.176	.148	.127	.106	.092	.078

FACTORS OWNERS CANNOT INFLUENCE

Certain factors are out of an owner's control and the following
can affect the same customer differently each time they drink.
Training servers to watch for visual cues of intoxication from the
BAC chart means that they can adjust service.

Rate of Consumption

As the liver can only process one drink per hour, a guest
who consumes multiple drinks within an hour risks alcohol
stacking up in the bloodstream, much like a series of planes
circling an airport. As each hour of drinking goes by, more
and more alcohol stacks up.

For example, Joe enters your bar and drinks three beers over the course of two hours, or one drink every forty minutes. His table would look like this:

Hour	Drink In	Drink Out	Net Drinks in Bloodstream
1	1.5	1	0.5
2	1.5	1	1
3	0	1	0

When Joe leaves, he has the equivalent of one drink still in his bloodstream. One hour after he leaves, the alcohol will finally metabolize out.

Sam enters your bar and drinks six beers over the course of two hours, or one drink every twenty minutes. His table would look like this:

Hour	Drink In	Drink Out	Net Drinks in Bloodstream
1	3	1	2
2	3	1	4
3	0	1	3
4	0	1	2
5	0	1	1
6	0	1	0

When Sam leaves, he has the equivalent of four drinks still in his bloodstream and may be legally drunk—depending upon his size and your state's BAC limits. It will take him four hours to metabolize the alcohol before it's completely out of his system.

If Joe and Sam are sitting next to one another, Sam should start exhibiting the signs of intoxication much faster than Joe.

Assuming they both weigh about 220 pounds, their relative BAC levels are as follows:

	Joe	Sam
BAC First Hour	0.009	0.018
BAC Second Hour	0.002	0.070

Joe, according to the chart, would probably be loosening his tie at the end of the second hour, while Sam could be showing marked lapses in judgment and his coordination may be impaired. Obviously, while Sam is not legally drunk, his driving ability would be impaired.

Customer drinking rates—how fast they drink—have a major impact on how intoxicated customers get. Bar owners who want to have customer-friendly yet legally responsible bars will try to influence this rate in any way possible through strategies listed in the second section of this book.

Binge Drinking

Binge drinking is where a customer drinks very rapidly in a short period to increase the effects of alcohol. Binge drinking, much like Sam's rate of consumption in the previous example, will produce signs of intoxication at a much faster rate since the drinker is purposely allowing alcohol to stack up in the bloodstream. Binge drinking is popular with college students, especially those who are underage, and when they turn 21, they may continue this practice when entering the bar scene.

Body Fat

Alcohol can pass through muscle tissue but not through fat.

Therefore, leaner, athletically built customers may have a lower BAC than customers with more body fat, even though the two weigh the same.

Body Size

The bigger — and generally heavier — the customer, the more blood in their body. Therefore, drink for drink their BAC chart shows lower levels than that of a smaller person. This single factor dramatically affects BAC charts and how they are calculated for each person. Since it's rude to ask customers their weight, servers need to be able to size up a customer before checking a chart.

Age

The older people get, the more their enzymes and liver tend to slow down. Older patrons may also be on medication that affects how alcohol is absorbed.

Sex

Female hormones makes a difference to how the liver metabolizes alcohol. Women are also smaller and have more body fat than men of the same size.

Can I refuse to serve a pregnant customer?

Generally, no. A pregnant woman is capable of making her own decisions and bears the responsibility of her choices. Discriminating against a pregnant woman is sex discrimination, and a refusal to serve her means a possible lawsuit.

Secondly, how do you know she is pregnant? Unless she, or someone who knows for certain, has told you, your customer may just be overweight, or she may have a tumor or growth or be carrying a fanny pack in front.

Medications

Most medications, both prescription and over the counter, will interfere with the metabolism of the alcohol, or the alcohol will cancel out the benefits of the medication. If someone is on medication, they should not consume alcohol without their doctor's consent.

Unfortunately, you cannot ask your customers for detailed printouts from their pharmacy before serving them. If you see a customer taking pills at the bar or looking under the weather, a careful caution may be in order.

Drugs

Illegal drugs affect the absorption rate of alcohol. Some will slow the metabolism down, while other illegal drugs combined with alcohol will cause drowsiness and a possible loss of consciousness. Treat all customers who look "high" when they arrive as being intoxicated.

Level of Happiness

A customer who is calm and happy will probably have a lower BAC rate than a guest who is upset. In some cases, the emotional disturbance may be from outside the bar — loss of job or a family crisis, for example, and they are seeking alcohol for solace. These customers may need a shoulder to cry on instead of further drinks. Sometimes the disturbance is from inside the bar — the home team is losing — and the customer needs a gentle reminder to keep things in perspective.

Managing the customer's consumption by using the factors listed above will help you to create your responsible beverage service.

CHAPTER 1 MANAGER'S TO-DO CHECK SHEET

- Make copies of all of the BAC charts.

- Hang them up in the bar.

- Give copies to all employees.

BLOOD *ALCOHOL* CONTENT CHART

FEMALE

Percentage of alcohol in bloodstream based on weight and consumption.

Weight	1	2	3	4	5	6	7	8	9
100	.05	.09	.14	.18	.23	.27	.32	.36	.41
120	.04	.08	.11	.15	.19	.23	.27	.30	.34
140	.03	.07	.10	.13	.16	.19	.23	.26	.29
160	.03	.06	.09	.11	.14	.17	.20	.23	.26
180	.03	.05	.08	.10	.13	.15	.18	.20	.23
200	.02	.05	.07	.09	.11	.14	.16	.18	.20
220	.02	.04	.06	.08	.10	.12	.14	.17	.19
240	.02	.04	.06	.08	.09	.11	.13	.15	.17

NUMBER OF DRINKS CONSUMED IN 1 HOUR OF TIME

1 DRINK = 12 oz. Beer • 3 oz. of Wine • 1 oz. of Spirits

FACT: .08% Is Legally Drunk In Most States

Alcohol Awareness & Prevention

© 2005 Atlantic Publishing Group, Inc. • Item #BACF-PS to re-order please call 1-800-814-1132

ALCOHOL AWARENESS POSTER: Blood Alcohol Content Chart—Female
Posters are printed in full color and laminated to reduce wear and tear. It measures 11" x 17". Available from Atlantic Publishing, Item # BACF-PS, $9.95. Blood Alcohol Content Chart—Male is also available (Item # BACM-PS). To order, call 1-800-814-1132 or visit www.atlantic-pub.com.

CHAPTER 2

SERVING ALCOHOL AND THE LAW

A mericans have been regulating alcohol service since the first Europeans came ashore. Tavern owners in colonial times underwent an examination, much like applying for a liquor license today, before they were allowed to open their premises. They had to be of good moral character and agree to local traditions before the tavern could be built. Tavern owners also had to deal with local law officials who would check in to see if the crowd was under control. They faced hearings with local magistrates, and when family members complained that someone was drinking too much, relatives could have customers banned from the premises. In short, not much has changed in two hundred years as far as the legal supervision of taverns is concerned.

What has changed is the relationship between a tavern owner and their customers as far as responsibility for over-consumption is concerned. In the days of King George, if a patron had too much to drink and fell off their horse, the worst they would risk was death from exposure or a broken limb. Because most of the damage was to the person who had been drinking, the view was that they were responsible, not the tavern owner who merely served them the drink. Today, the consequences of drinking are more likely to involve the general community rather than just the consumer. A patron who drinks and then drives puts the general population at risk from behind the wheel.

Another issue with drinking and the public began to surface with the rise of modern medicine. Scientists and doctors were able to map the workings of the mind and body and precisely measure how alcohol affects a person, even after just one drink. They proved that consumption equates to diminished capacity, making the drinker less able to act responsibly toward themselves and the community. Thus, the responsibility for preventing problems with alcohol consumption slowly began to shift from the individual drinker to the server, who, being sober, could keep track of what was going on.

As awareness of diminished capacity and increased accidents came into play, innocent victims of alcohol began to seek legal redress from the tavern owner, rather than the drinker. Before the passage of specific laws, a person injured by a drunk could only sue the drunk for damages. As most drinkers did not have the money to compensate for damage caused, the legal system began to look at where they purchased their alcohol for redress. Moreover, as motor vehicles, complex machinery, and other societal factors arose, tavern owners began to face restrictions regarding serving people to the point that the local community risked harm.

Cars usually come to mind when discussing drunk driving, but operators of motorized boats, wheelchairs, and scooters all have been arrested and successfully prosecuted for driving under the influence of alcohol. If it has a motor and is drivable, it is fair game for prosecution under these laws.

Before Prohibition, most states began passing a series of laws collectively called "dram shop" statutes. Those laws codified who could own and operate a tavern, and licensing of owners began. The laws also moved the responsibility for consumption from the customer to the server, allowing those who had been injured to collect from the tavern owner. Depending on the state, the laws could be extremely harsh or designed to prevent frivolous lawsuits against the owner. This patchwork of laws existed up until Prohibition.

After the Twenty-First Amendment was passed, canceling Prohibition, the responsibility for laws regulating the service of alcohol returned to the states. Since Prohibition had nullified those laws, some states took advantage and redesigned their laws, while others simply re-enacted their pre-Prohibition statutes. Today federal highway funds are withheld from states that have not enacted or enforced a law that provides that a person with a BAC of .08 or greater commits an offence when operating a motor vehicle and enforced a legal drinking age of 21. Otherwise, each state is responsible for designating proper and customary legal norms for service within their boundaries.

Thirty-six states have enacted dram shop laws during the post-Prohibition era. The remaining 14 states have not adopted them, but have legislation on the books that mirror dram shop principles. The Appendix shows each state's status and other applicable statutes that affect current-day tavern owners. Since each state can also pass the responsibility for serving alcohol to their respective counties, cities, or other local jurisdictions, this creates even more confusion regarding applicable standards. It is strongly recommended that an owner check with their legal advisor concerning applicable regulations for their operation.

WHAT ARE DRAM SHOP LAWS?

Dram shop laws refer to a series of regulations passed by individual states to regulate the service of alcohol. While most dram shop laws are similar, there are differences between each state's statutes reflecting when the laws were passed, the state's history with alcohol, and local customs. In general, dram shop states usually have laws stating:

- That the server of alcohol and the owner/manager of the establishment have a responsibility to the general public to prevent an individual from becoming intoxicated.

- That an operation should not serve those who are underage in their establishment.

Together, these two concepts put the burden on the owner to monitor their patrons' consumption and to take the necessary steps to prevent problems. In a dram shop state, someone who sells liquor to either a conspicuously inebriated person or to a minor, may face criminal misdemeanor charges in addition to a civil lawsuit. Criminal charges may be filed against the server, the manager, and the owner, even if the latter two were not on the premises when the incident occurred. The owner, manager, and server may also face fines. Third-party victims are permitted by statute to sue the bar server, owner, and manager for any and all damages that they have received because of an inebriated person. It is your responsibility as an owner to ensure that you are protected from such claims.

COMMON LAW STATES

If you are not in a dram shop state, then the concept of negligence may apply to your establishment. Under current negligence practices, if a "reasonable person" could foresee a problem, you are liable for damages. A parallel food service example is, "If the floor is wet, then patrons could slip and injure themselves, leaving the restaurant liable for medical bills. Therefore, a restaurant should mark when a floor is wet so to prevent falls and lawsuits." The corresponding alcohol service assumption may be that a "reasonable" person could see that a drunken patron driving home may cause themselves or someone else harm, and so they should not be allowed to drive. This has been expanded by a variety of court cases in this area to enforce prevention of intoxication by customers in a bar, something along the lines of an "If they are not drunk, then they cannot harm anyone" principle.

In general, in a common law state, innocent third parties may have restrictions on their ability to sue the bar owner. At present, all third parties can sue the patron who caused the damage, and in turn, that patron can sue the bar for allowing them to leave in such condition. Some states will allow legal redress or insurance claims by the third party directly against the bar under certain circumstances.

Whether you are in a dram shop or common law state, the result is the same: bar owners are legally prohibited from selling to minors and should minimize the effects of alcohol upon the community.

WHO ARE THE PARTIES?

Most states allow a variety of people to check your operation and serving policies. Local law enforcement representatives can visit your premises while you are open and monitor how you serve your patrons. In addition, they can create "undercover" stings where a minor attempts to purchase a drink, and if they succeed, an immediate shutdown of your bar may result.

The courts recognize several distinct "parties" as being able to sue or press charges against the bar. The first party is your patron: the person who did the drinking. If they are a minor or became intoxicated at your premises and caused themselves harm, such as falling down the stairs, they can sue you for damages. In some states, a legal-aged first party may have limits placed on how much they can collect, as those states feel a drinker has some responsibility for their own actions. In the case of a minor, most states will allow the parent to sue as the child's legal guardian.

The second group that can sue you is known as "third-party litigants": they did not drink at your establishment, but the person who did caused them harm. Most third-party litigants will sue, as they have damages or bills that were caused by the drinker. Third-party lawsuits can include property damage to houses, yards, mailboxes and cars; medical reimbursements for hospital and doctor's care; rehabilitation; lost wages; pain and suffering; and, in the case of death, damages related to loss of income for dependants. In a dram shop state, third-party litigants are able to sue once they prove their basic case; in common law states they may have to petition the courts for findings on a criminal case, which will be followed by a civil suit for damages. Liquor liability insurance for an establishment may cover part of these bills, but an owner will still have to pay out-of-pocket expenses as well as possibly face a substantial increase in premiums if the policy is renewed.

In some states your employees may be able to sue you as well, especially if they can document that your establishment had a cavalier attitude toward minors or if you overruled a server who shut off service to a customer who later caused an accident. You may be liable for their legal costs in the main lawsuit.

Who is who?

Tom owns the Campanari Inn. Danielle, his best bartender, serves Girard ten beers over the course of two hours. On his way home, Girard crashes his truck into a car driven by Tony. Tony is killed, and Girard is critically wounded. Janna, Tony's wife, decides to sue.

In this case, Janna and Tony are the "third parties." On her behalf and on the behalf of Tony's estate, Janna can sue Tom the owner, Danielle the server, and Girard the driver. If the accident occurs in a dram law state, Janna can sue all three under the particular dram shop code. In a non-dram shop state, Janna can sue Girard, but her ability to sue Tom and Danielle would be based on local case law and precedents.

Regardless of whether the accident happened in a dram shop state or a non-dram shop state, Girard may also be able to sue Tom and Danielle for compensation for his injuries. Some dram shop states will limit the amount that Girard can collect, or he may have to prove that Tom and Danielle were extraordinarily lax in their monitoring of his drinking. If it is a non-dram shop state, Girard may still be able to sue for damages depending upon the circumstances of his drinking: if he can show that a reasonable person would think that he was impaired when he left, then Tom and Danielle may still be liable.

Danielle may be able to sue Tom if she can show that his particular business practices left her legally vulnerable. For example, if of the ten beers she served Girard, four of them were free drinks given to him by Tom, then she may be able to shift some of her legal responsibility to Tom.

BAR HOPPING?

Some customers like to "bar hop"; that is, start at one establishment and move on to several others during the course of an evening. They could drink one or two drinks within an hour, leave, go to the next bar, and repeat the sequence. After a few hours, they may be legally drunk, yet not visibly intoxicated to servers. Since they are only having one or two drinks in your establishment, they may not trigger any concerns based on counting drinks.

If an accident happens, law enforcement will document the approximate times of the visit and interview to find out how much they drank. Any bar that served the customer drinks can be part of the litigation; the court will look usually look to the later bars for legal responsibility and remedies. In this situation, observing customers — before they order — is the most important legal defense. If they show any sign of intoxication or make comments, such as they just left a neighboring establishment, then that should be a red flag for servers to exercise caution with them. If they arrive at your bar under the influence of alcohol, they should be denied entrance and alternative transportation should be arranged for them.

RESPONSIBLE BEVERAGE SERVICE IS GOOD BUSINESS PRACTICE

Following dram shop laws is good business practice in all localities. As a bar owner, you employ local people, and for the most part, serve local customers. A bar with a dubious reputation for serving minors or drunks will generally not attract an ongoing clientele. The vast majority of bars will find it difficult to survive without the patronage of responsible, legal-aged patrons in their area — people who just want a drink and a good time. Furthermore, a bar with a "reputation" will invite further visits from law enforcement, continuing the erosion of clientele. It is better to stay on the side of caution — serving drinks within prescribed laws.

WHAT DO AUTHORITIES LOOK FOR?

Even if you are generally a responsible owner, sometimes all it takes is a complaint or a sting to have officials look at what you are doing and how you follow applicable laws. Most law enforcement and liquor authorities look to see if you are trying your best to cut down on incidents. The key is to create an atmosphere that shows you are practicing responsible business practices. Most of the next section of this book is dedicated to helping a bar owner create such an atmosphere within their operation.

Key practices include:

Staffing:

- Employ enough people to monitor and serve your expected clientele.

- Carefully hire and train your personnel.

- Have an alcohol-training program, highlighting the

medical and legal consequences of drinking.

- Have the training program show employees how to handle the most common problems with serving alcohol.

- Train all servers and door people how to identify minors and how to avoid serving them in your establishment.

- Train all servers and door people how to identify intoxicated patrons and avoid serving them in your establishment.

- Have control and disciplinary procedures in effect, to show that you are serious with your employees.

- Have written policies and procedures in the establishment.

- Have all servers sign to confirm that they have received training, and have those records on hand.

- Prohibit drinking on the job and create policies for off-duty employees and their drinking during off hours.

For your establishment:

- Actively promote your establishment based on activities, ambience, or clientele, rather than on aggressive drinking promotions.

- Promote nonalcoholic beverages and food as part of your establishment.

- Have alternative transportation methods available for your patrons to prevent driving after drinking.

- Encourage patrons to not become intoxicated by taking steps to keep them sober.

- Create an operation where drinking is part of the fun, not the main focus of your business.

Section II will focus on setting up your establishment, while Section III will focus on employee training plans.

OTHER LEGAL ISSUES

Most states have enacted several other laws, which, while not directly related to alcohol service, may have significant impact on your establishment. Violating these laws usually results in some sort of penalty, either financial or in terms of points against your liquor license, which can be used to deny renewal. Violations of these items also invite further inspection into your business practices and how you are trying to prevent problems. The usual assortment of state laws includes the following:

Legal Serving, Pouring, and Selling Age

While you have to be 21 in order to drink alcohol, various states allow employees younger than 21 to do certain tasks. Some states allow a minor to take an order (write on a pad that this customer wants a beer), to convey (take the bottle over to a table), to pour (pour the wine into the glass), or to sell (collect money or sell tickets for drinks).

Legal Age for Entry in an Alcohol Service Establishment

Depending upon your alcohol license, some states restrict minors from entering the dedicated bar area. If you have a restaurant with a liquor license, all states allow minors into restaurant seating areas, but some will restrict access by minors to a separate bar area.

Hours of Operation and Service

Every local liquor license board establishes the time range during the day when alcohol may be served. You can set your own hours of operation, but you cannot serve alcohol during forbidden times. In some areas, the sale of alcohol on Sundays may be severely curtailed.

Promoting Alcoholic Drinks Through "Happy Hours"

Many states, counties, and municipalities prohibit promotional activities, such as "happy hours," where the consumption of alcohol is heavily promoted.

> The Appendix shows if your state has any of these laws. You will need to check if your local county and/or municipality have passed laws that override state guidelines.

The usual restrictions include the following:

- Serving two or more drinks at a time to a patron.

- Providing unlimited drinks for a flat price.

- Discounting drinks based on a special day of the week or an hour of the day.

- Providing cocktails or mixers containing a higher content of alcohol than normal for the same price.

- Offering champagne or wine bottles or any other alcoholic beverages as prizes to a patron at your establishment.

In general, you can market specific times as special occasions, for example, every Wednesday night, serving free appetizers from 5 p.m. to 7 p.m. as "Over the Hump Day," as long as you don't discount the price of the drink or restrict food to customers who order drinks.

Signage Requirements

Most states require signs to be posted prominently and be included on your printed menus (if you have them) concerning various topics. Sign topics could include the following:

- The effect of alcohol on the body.

- The effect of alcohol on a fetus for pregnant women.

- The effect of smoking on the body.

- Hours of operation.

- Prices of drinks and their alcohol content.

- Food available.

- Cab services.

- How long or thoroughly meat items must be cooked.

- Bounced check fees.

- Copies of liquor license, food license, sanitation inspections, and bartender licenses.

Bartender Licenses/Operator Licenses

In addition to a liquor license specific to the location, some states require all bartenders to have their own bartender license. That particular license is attached to the person and not the bar that employs them. Therefore, when they are employed at another premise, they take the license with them. Some states also require managers to have a separate license. There may be various combinations of law concerning how many operator versus bartender licensed personnel need to be on the premises at all times.

Server Training

Some states require that all servers undergo alcoholic beverage service training, and some even go as far as specifying the exact format of training or approved trainers. States that make these requirements usually legislate certain topics to be covered during training, the format of the training, the length of the training class, and may also dictate certain test questions. States may additionally dictate certain philosophical wordings that can be anti-alcohol in nature.

Mandatory Insurance

Some states require that you have specific insurance to cover your responsibilities to serve alcohol, over and above your general business insurance. They may also require performance bonds, posted each year when your liquor license is renewed, to cover the average cost of a lawsuit in order to prevent you from declaring bankruptcy in the case of an incident.

CHAPTER 2 MANAGER'S TO-DO CHECK SHEET

- Check the Appendix for my state laws.

- Check with local legal counsel concerning local laws that might affect my establishment.

- Get a copy of our liquor license and find the local codes that govern it.

- If in a dram shop state, get a copy of the fines and penalties imposed for serving someone who is a minor or intoxicated.

MANAGEMENT RESPONSIBILITIES WHEN SERVING ALCOHOL

WHO NEEDS TO READ THIS SECTION?

This section is for owners and managers of establishments that hold liquor licenses. It addresses topics that only those in authority can change, as opposed to those related to a server who follows directions. This section covers the marketing, service, and delivery aspects of serving alcohol. Local legal advice should be consulted regarding any changes.

3

FIND YOUR TARGET CUSTOMERS

Part of the fun of bar hopping is going around and looking at what type of people visit different bars — obviously Hooters will have a much different clientele than the lounge at the local Sheraton Hotel. Defining your ideal client will help you to create policies based on whom you are serving, rather than on general situations, which might not fit your operation.

Who are your regular customers? How old are they? Are they retired, professional, blue collar, white collar, or unemployed? Do they come by themselves or in groups? Do you get dating couples or friends traveling in pairs? What do they drink, and how often does your sale mix change? Understanding who your customers are goes a long way toward creating a training plan.

For example, which bar needs to worry about checking IDs and keeping minors out: a bar located next to the local senior center filled with retired professionals or the college bar located on a strip on the busy side of the town? Obviously, while both need to be vigilant, the manager near the college needs to be more worried about checking IDs, as that bar is more likely to attract minors. As an owner, you need to watch whom you are serving and how you are serving them, as this is an important part of creating a training program.

The key to this is to find a target market and create an atmosphere that draws and keeps customers in. By clearly defining whom you want, you can then make changes to support them. For example, the target market could be:

> Twenty-five to thirty-five-year-old professionals, college educated, work in surrounding legal and financial offices. Will come here directly from work. Mostly single; want to unwind.

What comes to mind? Can you hear music playing? What do they drink? How are they dressed? By clearly defining your target market, you can create strategies to keep them from overdrinking and know where your problem areas will arise.

Another example:

> Forty to seventy years old, predominantly male, blue collar, limited income. Usually visit the bar twice a week for a few hours. They are careful with their money. Retired patrons will come in the morning, others after work, especially after first shift ends. Many are working construction and other weather-dependent jobs, so bad weather means good business for this bar.

Now what comes to mind? What is the sex of the bartender?

How are they dressed? How many beers do you think they will have in their few hours at the bar? Why are they coming to the bar?

By clearly defining your market, you can reduce your dram shop liabilities. For example, in the first case, patrons want to unwind quickly, so having drink recipes that slow the effect of alcohol will help. Playing dance music will keep them moving and slow their drinking. Putting out plates of free food will help keep them from over-consuming.

For the second bar, are they coming to drink or to get out of the house? Patrons in this type of establishment could be lonely, and a bartender who listens to them goes a long way in slowing down their drinking. Another suggestion would be to keep this group entertained with card games or TV shows.

RISK

Risk assessment is simply taking a good look at your operation and trying to figure out where you are vulnerable. Working through the issue and solving it in a timely manner within your operation will help your long-term business.

Why do people go to a bar? Alternatively, why do people go to *your* bar? Customers choose a bar based on location, ambiance, available activities, reputation, recommendation, price/value relationship, range of drinks available, and service. Most bars attract two main groups of people: regulars who visit the establishment on a frequent basis and people who may come once or twice during a season. Your goal is to create a customer-friendly yet legally sound bar that brings them in, based on whom you are trying to attract.

OPERATIONAL ASSESSMENT QUIZ

Where are your problem areas? This quiz is designed to give you a sense of potential problem areas. Don't worry; there aren't any grades involved.

Part I—Clientele

1. Most of my customers are:

    a. World War II veterans.

    b. Baby boomers.

    c. Generation X.

    d. Barely legal.

2. When customers come in, they tend to be:

    a. By themselves.

    b. Romantic couples.

    c. Same-sex couples or small groups (buddies).

    d. Large groups of both sexes.

3. If a stranger arrives by themself and sits at the bar:

    a. My regulars would talk to them.

    b. My regulars would say "hi."

    c. My regulars would glare at them.

4. Most of my customers are:

    a. Regulars.

    b. A mix of regulars and strangers.

    c. A different bunch every day.

5. When in my bar, customers usually:

    a. Sit and chat amongst their party.

    b. Play pool, darts, or watch TV.

    c. Listen to music and dance.

    d. They are all over the bar.

6. Customers coming to my bar:

    a. Know what to wear and won't come in unless dressed correctly.

    b. Most of my customers are dressed about the same.

    c. There is a wide range of clothing in my bar.

    d. What dress code?

7. What is our minor quotient?

    a. Minors are not allowed in, nor do they want to come in.

    b. Minors are allowed in because of the nature of our operation; for example, a pizza joint or restaurant, but we can identify them and card them.

    c. Minors consider us an attraction and try to get in and order from us.

    d. We are not sure how many minors are in the building, and whether or not they are served.

Part II—Bar Atmosphere

1. The lighting in my place is:

    a. So bright that you have to wear your shades.

    b. Just right; dark enough for atmosphere, yet bright enough to see everything.

    c. Pretty spotty; some areas are very dark and you can't see people very well.

d. We send the servers out with flashlights.

2. With no music playing, the noise level in my bar is:

   a. Quieter than a church.

   b. Some noise, but conversationally friendly.

   c. Noisy, but a table of customers can still hear each other talking.

   d. Huh? I can't hear you.

3. When the music is playing:

   a. It is quiet background music.

   b. It is bouncy, fun, sing-along type music.

   c. It is loud dance music and customers are out on the dance floor.

   d. The mosh pit is open for business.

4. Sitting on my barstools:

   a. Is comfortable for about an hour.

   b. Is comfortable for a couple of hours.

   c. Is so cushy that customers can fall asleep.

5. Sitting on chairs at tables:

    a. What chairs?

    b. Is comfortable for about an hour.

    c. Is comfortable for a couple of hours.

    d. Is so cushy that customers fall asleep.

6. If strangers walked into my bar, their first
    impression would be that my place is:

    a. A place for drinking, stimulating conversation,
       and quiet music.

    b. A place to meet a bunch of friends before going
       somewhere else.

    c. A place to sit and drink for several hours.

    d. A happening place with lots going on.

7. Within my immediate neighborhood (walking
    distance):

    a. My bar is the only place that serves alcohol.

    b. There are a couple of places around, but we
       serve different types of customers.

    c. Sometimes it is hard to tell where my bar ends

and the next one begins.

Part III—Offerings

1. Someone orders vodka on the rocks, I give them a choice of:

    a. Several imported top-shelf vodkas.

    b. We have top-shelf and well items.

    c. We have a well and couple of calls.

    d. We've got vodka—take what we have.

2. In general, my sales mix is:

    a. Mostly beer.

    b. Mostly beer with a healthy dose of cocktails.

    c. Quite a few cocktails.

    d. Lots of shots and shooters.

3. When I sell beer, I sell:

    a. Only by the glass.

    b. Mostly by the glass, some pitchers.

    c. About half glasses, half pitchers.

    d. All pitchers.

4. As far as trendy drinks are concerned:

    a. My customers stick to their favorites.

    b. We sell mostly local favorites and occasional drinks that we need to look up the recipes.

    c. My customers only drink the most popular drinks available and demand them as a matter of course.

    d. My bar creates trends in drinks.

5. At my bar, customers can:

    a. Dance.

    b. Play pool, play darts, or participate in card games, contests, or conversation.

    c. Play computer gambling games.

    d. Sit.

6. I have:

    a. A full food service operation.

    b. A limited menu available at the bar.

    c. Pre-packaged snacks available: chips, beef jerky, etc., or I have pretzels, popcorn, and peanuts available.

    d. What food?

7. Food:

    a. If the bar is open, food is available.

    b. Food opens later or closes earlier than the bar.

    c. If you are going to a bar, why do you want food?

8. In terms of revenue:

    a. Food is primary; alcohol is secondary.

    b. Food and alcohol are about even.

    c. Alcohol is more important than food.

9. In terms of nonalcoholic beverages:

    a. We have a full line of nonalcoholic beers and wines with an extensive menu of nonalcoholic concoctions.

    b. We have nonalcoholic beers and wines and regular bar mixers, such as juices, sodas, and water.

c. We have water.

Part IV—How Drinks Are Served

1. A party of two women orders a strawberry margarita and a virgin strawberry margarita. The two drinks are served:

    a. In completely different glasses.

    b. In similar glasses, perhaps one has a tinted stem.

    c. In the same glasses, we use straws or garnishes to tell them apart.

    d. "Um, could you take a sip? One has the booze."

2. A party of two men orders a beer and a cola. Your price structure is:

    a. Charge for the beer, soda is free.

    b. Charge for the beer, soda is a minimal amount.

    c. The beer and soda are priced about the same.

    d. The soda is more expensive than the beer.

3. Another party of two men both order Scotch on the rocks. To make them, the bartender will:

    a. Use a computerized automatic pourer to make

the drinks.

b. Use automatic pour sytem to make the drinks.

c. Use pour nozzles and jiggers; their use is enforced.

d. One....two....three....four...

4. You have a party of four in your bar. Three are 22 and the fourth is a 20-year-old. You can tell what the minor is drinking because:

   a. Minors are served in different glasses and you put armbands on the non-legal-aged people.

   b. You give the minor a different-colored glass.

   c. You didn't take a drink order from the minor.

   d. There is a minor at that table?

5. It is a busy Saturday Night. Your doorman:

   a. Checks everyone's ID under bright lights and pulls off to the side all customers whose IDs need another look.

   b. Checks everyone's ID.

   c. Only checks IDs of the people who look young.

   d. They are too busy breaking up fights to check IDs.

Part V—Your Staff

1. Most of my staff has been with this place:

    a. Since it opened or for so long I can't remember when they were hired.

    b. I have a core crew that has been around for a while; the others tends to stay about a year or so.

    c. I have 100 percent turnover over the course of a year.

    d. I am always hiring new people.

2. Most of my staff are:

    a. Baby Boomers.

    b. Generation X.

    c. Barely legal to serve.

3. The staff that serve alcohol:

    a. Have extensive training on what each drink is, how it is made, and who is most likely to order it.

    b. Have some solid knowledge—can make most drinks and have been around long enough to know where to find a recipe.

    c. Know the well and what beer I serve.

    d. Are not sure that there is a difference between gin and vodka.

4. My staff communicate with each other:

    a. Very well; they keep each other informed on a regular basis.

    b. Somewhat well; there is the occasional snit.

    c. Not well at all; there is a lot of in-fighting.

    d. I don't think they know each other's names.

5. For training and documentation:

    a. My staff has undergone extensive training on serving alcohol, from a service point of view and from a point of view of monitoring intoxication level. They have also received and signed for written documentation that illustrate how it is done. We repeat this training on an annual basis.

    b. My staff has been through training and have copies of all of the documentation, but I usually wait until I get a big enough group together before I train them.

    c. My staff has had basic bar training.

d. What training?

6. If it is going to be a really busy Saturday night, for staffing I will have:

    a. The appropriate amount of staff for our operation, with an extra swing employee available.

    b. Barely the number I need for my operation, and if a few call in, I am in trouble.

    c. I am planning on pulling a station and everyone is working a double.

So how did you do? Add up each time you answered:

A. _____

B. _____

C. _____

D. _____

Results:

Mostly A's – "A" answers represent either the least risky situation or an overly idealized situation. "A" answers are idealized goals within prevention programs.

Mostly B's – "B" answers show medium-risk situations or

typical course of a bar owner. "B" answers tend to show the trade off between the cost of administrating an alcohol beverage program and the costs involved with having an acceptable program.

Mostly C's – "C" answers show riskier behavior by customers, staff and owners, coupled with some legally shaky beverage management issues. "C" answers need checking and modification to keep within responsible beverage service guidelines.

Mostly D's – "D" answers show the riskiest behaviors by your customers, staff and managers or illustrate serious management issues that need to be addressed.

The next few chapters in the book address the quiz questions and suggestions to modify your risks. Go back and circle your "C" and "D" answers, and find the section applicable to modify your risks. You should do this before you begin the server training programs, as these are the main areas that a manager should fix before servers are trained.

CHAPTER 3 MANAGER'S TO-DO CHECK SHEET

- Determine your target customers. Describe them in terms of sex, age, occupation, average check size, and what they like to do in a bar.

- Review quiz answers and highlight all "C" and "D" answers.

CHAPTER

TYPES OF OPERATIONS AND RESPONSIBLE BEVERAGE SERVICE

B ased on your type of operation, several special risk factors exist. Prudent management dictates that you minimize risks based on your establishment and type of licensure. This section will discuss the different types of bars and solutions to manage the service. Even if you own a "regular" bar, or only have a restaurant liquor license, read this section for possible ideas that you can use in your operation.

HOTEL BARS

The main difficulty with a hotel bar is the customer's argument that they are not driving and can therefore have more drinks. Despite the fact their staying in a hotel may minimize the possibility of their driving, once they leave the immediate bar area, you do not know where they are going or even if they return to their room. Furthermore, they may have guests with them who reside in the local area and are planning to return home after they leave. A hotel bar is still liable for injuries, such as tripping or falling as well as injuries to others on the property; for example, when an intoxicated guest knocks down another person. Do not encourage the attitude of "it's okay to get drunk" just because you manage a hotel bar. Treat hotel bars as if they were freestanding operations, and have the same training in place.

HOTEL ROOM SERVICE DELIVERY

In this situation, a customer orders and room service delivers bottles to the guest's room. If possible, a hotel should limit this type of service to mini bottles for liquor and single-serving bottles of beer and wine. Carefully price drinks to discourage room drinking in favor of the bar where visible consumption can be assessed. If mini bottles are not allowed by law, then a move to making the drinks and serving them in clear glass carafes, such as those used for hot water for tea, should help to control consumption.

A second issue is minors ordering alcohol either deliberately or as a joke. All room service attendants should be trained to check IDs and not deliver if a person of legal age is not in the room. Only one drink per legally aged person should be left in the room. Claims, such as "in the shower" or "down the hall" should be a caution that something is wrong and the delivery should not be made.

What happens if a guest of my hotel stops at a package store to bring their own alcohol in and then cause a problem? Is the hotel liable?

Generally, no. You cannot control what is in their luggage, nor can you inspect guests' bags when they check in. You also cannot control what happens behind closed doors. You can, however, enforce local occupancy laws (for example, two registered guests is not a party) and evict all non-guests from the establishment. You can respond to complaints from other guests and evict offenders based on noise and other factors. You can prohibit the consumption of alcohol in public places such as the lobby or the pool. But in general, activities behind closed hotel doors are considered legally similar to activities within the guest's own home, and as such, they are the ones who are liable.

HOTEL HOSPITALITY ROOM

Another common situation in hotels relates to the hospitality room, where a group is staying in the hotel and rents a suite with a bar setup for their members' use. In days gone by, the hotel would simply leave the alcohol, mixers, and glasses, and members would make their own drinks. The hosting organization would be responsible for monitoring consumption and preventing minors and those not associated with the group from drinking. Today, this setup is fraught with legal problems, as there is no way to monitor each individual guest's consumption. Leaving the responsibility to the host organization is also risky, as they might not want to "cut off" a member of their group.

Sell hospitality bars with a staff bartender and only for specified hours. Position the bartender as a solution, rather than an additional cost, by stressing that the organization has someone to take care of their needs while the party is going on.

TEMPORARY LICENSES

While they are described legally under various terms, temporary licenses usually fall under the same guidelines as fully fledged liquor licenses. For example, if you are a church, seeking a one-day permit to sell beer at a church picnic, you are subject to the same laws as a regular liquor license-holder in your town. Even as a temporary holder, who does not normally make money from the sale of alcohol, you will be required to fulfill general requirements concerning minors and selling/giving alcohol to intoxicated persons. It may be prudent to work with a local bar or restaurant and have them serve the alcohol if possible.

If you are serving outdoors, you may be required to "fence" off the alcohol. Work with your local law enforcement representative to ascertain the required number of entrances and exits. Make the fence see-through so that staff can see what is going on, yet dense enough so that drinks cannot go through. Work with your vendors to find unique glasses for alcohol, so if they are found in the general area, they can be confiscated. Finally, only allow legal-aged patrons in and have a doorman carefully check identification. Stamp hands, and only allow one drink per purchase to avoid over-consumption.

IN-HOUSE CATERING

A legal gray area exists for caterers who are working a party in a private home. No laws, except those in dry counties, prohibit a host from serving alcohol in their own house. In general, if someone is entertaining and serves alcohol to a guest, who then goes out and causes damage to themselves or to a third party, most states have statutes that hold the host liable to an extent. If a host serves a minor, other than their own child, they may also be liable for damages. With caterers, both professional and serious amateurs, the danger comes when the host asks you to set up the bar and/or serve the guests drinks. In most states, this area becomes extremely murky as you — the caterer — may be held to commercial dram shop laws, or you may be considered to be an employee who is obeying a host's requests. Seek legal advice if, as a caterer, you are planning to perform this service.

CATERING AND BANQUETS WITH MULTIPLE BAR SETUPS

Another issue that frequently arises in catering is in large group events, such as weddings or business functions, where multiple bars are needed. Guests circulate throughout the venue ordering drinks at more than one place. Managing this situation can be tricky, as an intoxicated guest may be denied service at one bar, yet get drinks at another bar. The facility and/or the caterers serving are still liable even though it is hard to keep track of guests.

To reduce risks:

- Try to concentrate the bars near each other, or within sightlines of each other—all bars can see at least two other bars so that intoxicated guests can be easily pointed out.

- Rent radios or walkie-talkies to help with communication. Have at least one bartender in a bar responsible for monitoring communication. Remember that guests may overhear the conversations, so keep the chatter down and restricted to the business at hand. Be careful how you describe guests, and do not use derogatory terms for them. Simple phrasing could include:

    "This is Bar A, we are 86'ing a white male, about six feet tall, mid-forties with gray/brown hair. He is wearing a black jacket with red shirt and black pants. Last seen heading toward Bar B. Bar B, do you have him in sight?"

- In addition to helping identify intoxicated individuals, bartenders can use this system to request additional stock, glasses and supplies, increasing the efficiency of the operation.

Who wants to wear a tacky wristband while dressed up for a wedding or bar mitzvah? The solution is to turn the wristband from an identifier into a party favor. Several online companies will make paper or silicon wristbands with an imprinted logo of your establishment, or the names of the honorees. Colors can be ordered to match bridesmaids' dresses, and setup costs for small runs (under one hundred) are surprisingly affordable. Lead-time is generally under a week, although they should be ordered once a deposit has been made. Build the price of the custom wristbands into the pricing structure for your alcohol service, and create a unique marketing memento for your customers and their guests.

- Train servers and bussers who mingle with guests how to identify intoxicated individuals. When serving food or cleaning tables, they are the eyes of the operation, whereas bartenders are usually stationary. If they see any behavior that concerns them, they can report it to the nearest bar. Alternatively, have the bars located near entrances for food service and trash removal, so that as the servers come in, they can quickly identify potential problems.

- Use common sense when serving. If the crowd is large enough, someone may need to get two drinks: one for themselves and one for their guest. Do not leave service trays around where customers can use them or they will order many drinks under the guise of serving the table. Most customers can only safely carry two to three drinks at a time without a tray.

Large social occasions also bring the problem of minors. If an event is being booked with minors, obviously or potentially present, then the sales manager needs to discuss the issue with the host before the event. Ask the host to remind legal-aged guests to bring identification, and once checked, issue wristbands for legal-aged guests—who will not take them off—in order for them to be able to drink. Servers and bartenders should double check identification when a drink is ordered to prevent IDs from being handed over before the party starts. If the party features "virgin" and "non-virgin" drinks, such as frozen strawberry slushies and strawberry margaritas, then they should be served in completely different glasses so that the glass- alcohol-wristband relationship should be readily apparent. Nearby empty glasses on tables should be removed before any minor is caught "sipping." Remove bottles of wine or champagne placed on the table for toasts as soon as that part of the event is over.

The bride is underage?

While checking identification when taking a check for the deposit, you learn that the bride is twenty, and will still be twenty on her wedding day. This can create a problem, as serving an underage guest, even if she is the bride, means that you are liable and in violation of state laws.

Long before the wedding day, you will need to discuss this issue with her and the fact that you cannot serve her alcohol. Some alternatives would be sparkling cider for champagne and nonalcoholic wine for table service, but the bride and groom need to realize that serving her is not an option.

AIRPORT BARS

It is understandable if after September 11, 2001, passengers want to seek comfort in a bottle before a plane ride, but airlines are cracking down on inebriated passengers flying, as they are a potential hazard in the air. Additionally, with security lock-downs and searches, customers who have layovers may be in the bar simply because of the lack of other options in terminal areas. At any sign of inebriation, passengers risk denial of boarding by gate attendants, so an airport bar must be extremely careful in serving customers.

Some suggestions for this situation include posting signs visible to all, stating the consequences of inebriation and boarding procedures. The sign could read, "Please understand that your airline could deny you seating on your flight if you appear intoxicated. Please monitor your consumption, as we would not wish your flight plans to be cancelled." If need be, the bartender or server could repeat this to customers as they order their drinks.

Another suggestion would be to add amusements to the bar area that entertain bored customers, without adding alcohol to the mix. Board and card games set out, karaoke and music, "fuzzy ball" kiddy dart games, personal movie and TV rentals, and computer games located adjacent to a serving area help to alleviate boredom without sacrificing airport security. Bar owners and managers in this situation need to work with airlines and airport managers to create activities in the terminal that keep patrons from simply drinking while waiting for their flight.

Finally, Department of Transportation rules strictly forbid pilots and other flight attendants from drinking before flying. Report any uniformed personnel in your bar who are drinking to the airport manager. Do not serve them any alcohol—even if they are coming off a flight. If they are simply waiting in your bar, without drinking, encourage airport management to create a comfortable employee waiting area that will not compromise the airline's reputation.

STADIUMS AND ARENAS

In light of a recent court case that held a company responsible for serving an intoxicated customer in a stadium setting, serving alcohol at large venue events should be reviewed. In these situations, several thousand people may be at a sporting event or concert with multiple bars across several floors in play. Like banquet situations that might have many guests, arenas serve far more people than normal, and they are much more mobile within a building. Additionally, concession workers may serve beer directly to customers in their seats from shoulder boxes. In this situation, monitoring guests is next to impossible. Some suggestions to counter this include:

- Assign floor concessionaires to specific areas within the building, and do not allow them to migrate to different locations. That way they can try to monitor and limit sales to inebriated patrons within their area. When floor concessionaires migrate, they will go where they think the most drinkers are, resulting in some customers receiving many drinks during the course of the event.

- Use careful service hours. Starting a half hour before the event starts and stopping about one hour before it ends can help alleviate inebriation and allow time for the alcohol to be processed. Some suggested stop times include:

    - Baseball: after the seventh inning

    - Football and basketball: after the third quarter

    - Hockey: after halftime

    - Plays, operas or story events: after the intermission

    - Musical events: about ten minutes into the headliner act

- Only allow a maximum of two drinks per person to be sold and no pitchers. If members of a group want a drink, then they all need to stand in line.

- Price drinks to discourage over-consumption. Factor in the cost of tickets and average food concessions to create a target price for the drinks. By making intoxication expensive, customers will tend to stay sober.

- Have and enforce security procedures that don't allow alcohol to be brought in from outside the building.

While you may wish to continue tailgating traditions, do not allow guests to bring in their own drinks into the main part of the building.

- Keep to beer and wine, which have more volume of liquid per ounce of alcohol; this way people will slow down their consumption to avoid having to use the restrooms. Limit beer to a 20-ounce cup and wine to an 8-ounce cup for service.

- For skyboxes, restaurants and bars in the building enforce no-alcohol-leaves-the-room policies. Hold those patrons to the same standards as freestanding bars. Do not have bar setups without a staff bartender in the room to make and serve drinks and monitor consumption.

- When shutting down a bar, shut it down completely. Close the security window to prevent customers from seeing the cleanup and requesting more alcohol. Lock all dispensing devices and coolers immediately so there is no temptation to continue selling.

- For tournaments where multiple games are held one after another with a clearing time between games, shut alcohol down before the fourth quarter of each game to allow those leaving time for the alcohol to metabolize. Plan to end alcohol sales for the night after the first half of the last game.

NIGHTCLUBS, PUBS, DANCE HALLS, DISCOS, ELECTRONIC MUSIC EVENTS

Whatever name they go by, these are the "happening" places in town, which might not see customers in until late in the evening. While the music may change from generation to generation, the operational aspects are still the same.

Of all of the categories of bars, this one is the most risky. This type of establishment usually has the most citations in a community simply because they were the last place someone had a drink, although it was not necessarily the place they drank the most. As such, most managers will face additional scrutiny from local law enforcement concerning these establishments.

Another area of concern is the sheer volume of people. It is not surprising to see over one thousand customers with "only" fifty bartenders and servers. In a place like this, no pretense is made to try to monitor drinks—it may simply be impossible.

Some suggestions:

- Bouncers are the most important line of defense with intoxicated guests. They need to check identification carefully and make sure that no drink-impaired people get past. Once in, if they are served—even if they do not drink—if something happens, your bar is the legally responsible party. Stress to your staff that intoxicated guests cannot enter the establishment.

- Before hiring bouncers, you need to perform a background check. Refuse employment to anyone with an assault or drug-selling conviction.

- Turn up the lights enough so that employees can see what is going on.

- Watch local density restrictions; the more people in an area, the more likely fights or other assaults will occur. Having too many people in one area can also make evacuation impossible in cases of fire or emergencies.

- Have a cover charge policy, especially for those who enter after 11 p.m. Charge everyone (no women free) to keep the amount of drinking down.

- Once a person has paid a cover charge, do not allow unlimited exiting and entering. Allow for one trip out and then mark the patron's hand with a permeable marker to show they have had their one exit. Multiple entrances and exits could indicate drug use or they are bringing in their own liquor.

- For drinks, stick to beer and wine; skip the shots, shooters, and other hard liquor drinks. Use the same guidelines as stadiums: 20 ounces for beer and 8 ounces for wine. One guest can only get a maximum of two drinks per order. Do not allow access to trays.

- Use a line management system, such as ropes, to mark areas to line up for drinks and access to bathrooms. By giving customers visual clues as to where to go and how to get a drink, they are more likely to take only one drink at a time.

- Ask a local cab company to create wall posters for their services. Install a direct line to their dispatcher for guests to use. Put posters in the lobby.

- Consider valet parking. Refuse to get the car if the patron appears intoxicated when they leave. Price parking so that it includes a "free" cab ride—the company can bill you later—and an overnight place for the car. Have your valets go through alcohol training as well.

THE STRIP

This is where, by zoning laws or local custom, virtually everyone with a liquor license in town ends up in one area. Once popular tools for community management, "strips" concentrate certain types of liquor licenses in one area for better policing ability. Strips face migratory customers who move from spot to spot based on many factors, with pricing being one of them. Strip bars also find it hard to differentiate themselves from their neighbors, as all bars seem to run together in the customer's mind. Bars in this situation may be owned by several people, yet are treated as one entity by their clientele and community.

Some suggestions:

- Face the obvious: As bar owners, you will need to meet

to discuss issues. Most owners are afraid of running into anti-trust laws, so the presence of a neutral third party in the room will take care of that. Neutral parties can be the local liquor commissioner, an official from your tavern association or restaurant association, or your local public health inspector. During the meeting, all bar owners need to agree on what times alcohol will be served, a mutual policy for warning each other about intoxicated customers, and not to admit intoxicated customers into the premises. Major holidays, such as Halloween, should be discussed well in advance as well.

- By not meeting and discussing these issues, bar owners face the risk of the local community lumping all bars together and punishing all for the sins of a few. By agreeing to some common mutually beneficial policies (except the pricing of individual drinks), bar owners in this situation can help each other to survive.

- Spend money on advertising, and create a niche. By creating a niche, you are seen as "different." Become the biker bar, health nut bar, alternative lifestyle bar, sports bar, dart and pool table bar, open mike comedy bar, or alternative music bar; whatever you decide, spend money and make your bar seen as that. For this area, hire a good marketing or advertising company to keep your message local, on target, and on people's minds. By creating a niche, you can target your establishment to those customers who will not mind spending a bit more for better service with like-minded customers. Niches can charge more and make more from their drinks, as they have a built-in clientele — and they can manage their regulars better than a bar with different customers each night. If you do not have a niche, you risk being lumped in with everyone else on the strip, thus increasing the risk that your business is dependent upon someone else's drunks migrating to your place.

• Consider paying your serving staff above the prevailing wages on the strip, especially if they stay past the probationary period. Staff who stay longer tend to be more comfortable with safer service techniques and usually have a "psychological buy-in" with the bar. Paying regular strip wages or below results in a higher turnover in staff, increasing your risk of problems. If higher wages are a financial issue, check out other alternatives, such as gift certificates, health insurance, or other benefits that your employees believe to be worthwhile.

A bar located on the strip in a college town did not have enough money to pay a higher hourly rate. Instead, the owner offered all of the servers and bartenders "house" rate on food purchases. That is, they placed their grocery orders with the bar's food service purveyor, and the bar owner guaranteed their money. The bar also kept the extra food, labeled in extra freezers, for those who could not fit it all in at home. The result: employees had cheaper food bills, and the bar had loyal employees.

CHAPTER 4 MANAGER'S TO-DO CHECK SHEET

- Order wrist bands.

- If you are a manager of one of the bars discussed, are all the suggestions listed a part of your usual operating procedures? If not, then fix the relevant parts.

- If you are a manager of a bar not discussed, find five suggestions that you can use in your establishment.

5

TYPES OF CUSTOMERS AND RESPONSIBLE BEVERAGE SERVICE

Different target customers will create different risks and require different ways to manage them. Places that have a higher percentage of minors, especially older teens and younger twenties, need different management techniques than those with an older clientele. How your customers come in — groups, solos, or couples — can make a difference to their consumption as well. Read on and mark the sections that will make a difference to you.

MINORS

Patrons under the age of 21 create special issues. In some states, depending on your type of license, they may not be allowed in the separate bar area. In most states, if you have a restaurant alcohol license, minors can be allowed within the food seating area. In other cases, such as banquet or catering operations, minors may be present within the group. In short, very few places serve alcohol where minors can be prohibited.

The issue then becomes one of identification and prevention of drinking. In some cases, such as a toddler in a high chair, identification and prevention should be a non-issue. The problem comes with teenagers and early twenty-year-olds (sixteen to twenty) who may look old enough to drink and may attempt to drink, but cannot be served. While checking identification is covered in the training section, identifying your "minor" quotient and taking preventative action may also be necessary. Some suggestions include:

- Prevent minors from entering after a designated time, such as 9 p.m., when food sales slow down, as having minors on the property after a certain hour increases the chance that they will gain access to alcohol.

- If your type of operation needs them, for example, a nightclub, have doormen who check ID before allowing entrance. The ID will need to be checked again by the server, but having a double-check will send the message that underage drinkers are not allowed.

- If you have doormen, have them check the ID of everyone; don't use an arbitrary level, such as below thirty, or forty years old. Checking everyone's ID means that the doorman is not guessing who is legal based on their dress and appearance.

The state of Wisconsin required everyone's ID to be checked. Many bars took the resulting publicity from having to card eighty-year-olds as a method of informing their customers that they had responsible beverage service policies.

To identify minors, look for the following:

- Trendy outfits, sports teams, or "hip" dress. To find what is considered trendy, simply save the department store circulars from Sunday papers to get a sense of what teenagers/early twenty-year-olds prefer to wear.

- Watch for ordering of "trendy" drinks: if it is popular in movies, TV shows, or teen-focused magazines, then underaged drinkers will try to order it.

- Underage drinkers also like sugary drinks, as they usually hide the harsh taste of alcohol. A run on ordering those types of drinks may indicate some underage patrons.

- Watch for customers who will not look employees in the eye; they will dodge eye contact by looking away, or in the case of couples, by hugging and holding hands.

- Watch for elaborate excuses or truly incredible tales for having a lack of identification:

  - "My wallet was stolen." (So shouldn't they be looking for it or calling the police?)

  - "I forgot my purse." (How are you driving without a license or coming in without money?)

  Usually minors will attempt to create elaborate stories in an attempt for a "sympathy" drink.

- Underage girls typically travel in packs, especially to nightclubs. One or two may be legal, but the rest aren't. Carefully check IDs when a pack shows up. You may also wish to jot down names and compare to see if two people with the same name come in.

- The hardest "forgeries" to catch are when a minor borrows ID belonging to a legal-aged sibling or other close relative. If they look alike, then such statements as "I got my hair cut/dyed," "I got glasses/contacts since that picture was taken" do sound reasonable and plausible. Usually what trips them up is their behavior in line or in the establishment: they are not acting like an older person, but are more immature. Quiz the candidate on details on their ID. Check the signature and ask for a second form of identification.

In short, minors tend to model their behavior in the bar from what they see on TV and in movies, as those are their only reference points. If you see patrons acting as if they are in a bad sitcom, then chances are they may be minors.

JUST LEGAL

The next main age group that bar owners needs to worry about is the "just legal" crew. Studies have shown that this group has been drinking alcohol for some time, probably in unregulated and unsupervised settings as dorm rooms, frat parties, raves, and private homes. The main issue with this age group is that they have not learned what is proper behavior in a bar and how to monitor their consumption in a responsible fashion. This group is the most likely to start fights and become violent within the establishment. Additionally, this group will binge drink. They consume as many drinks possible in a short amount of time, as that is how they learned to drink in unsupervised settings. If this group is your target market, then as a bar owner you need to:

- Check the IDs of the group carefully. Usually this group has underaged friends who are trying to get in with them.

- Insist on the one person/one drink rule. If they have to come to the bar to purchase alcohol, that will slow down their drinking.

- No pitchers or oversized drinks. Keep beer glasses to 20 ounces or below.

- Post signs on proper bar behavior, such as, "If you _____, then you will be asked to leave." Fill in with the most common occurrences in your bar.

- Count drinks carefully, and watch for over consumption in the first hour or so. Keep this group entertained with activities that will keep them from drinking.

OLDER PATRONS

The final age group bar owners need to keep a careful eye on is that of older patrons. As people age, their ability to metabolize alcohol is compromised, so chances are that an older person may show signs of intoxication faster than a similarly sized younger adult. Older customers are also more likely to be on medications that may affect their metabolism or react with alcohol, affecting their behavior. Finally, this group may simply be at your bar out of loneliness and wanting companionship. Monitor consumption carefully for this group.

HOW MANY ARE IN THE PARTY

How much a particular person will drink, depends on the amount of time that they spend in the bar and how fast they consume drinks. Most men, drinking at an average pace, consume one drink roughly every half an hour. Women are a little slower, taking 35 to 45 minutes a drink. Research shows that it usually does not matter how big the party is in terms of drinking, but the composition of the group and their purpose for coming to the bar is more important. A few key pointers have emerged:

- Solo drinkers will drink at their normal rate, but perceive themselves as being more intoxicated than if they are in a group. For example, when Sam drinks by himself, he begins to "feel" the alcohol after the second drink, yet when Sam comes in with his friends, it takes a few more drinks before he begins to "feel" the alcohol. Encourage your "bar patrons" to talk to each other to help slow the perception of inebriation.

- Because women drink more slowly than men, there

is a possibility that the server would rather "stack" women's drinks, rather than return to their tables ten minutes later to get their refills. Encourage servers to wait until the drink is nearly gone to offer a second round instead of getting the order after the man's drink is finished.

- Couples, on a romantic date versus buddies hanging around, will drink slightly less than their normal consumption. Work that in your favor by offering food for two to increase checks rather than move more drinks.

- Groups will usually drink the average number of drinks per hour, regardless of how large they are. Most of the time larger groups, as compared to couples or solos, are at your bar because of your activities. Be careful to aim refills for when most of the group is empty, rather than when the first customer is done.

DEALING WITH REGULARS

A regular is someone who visits you often enough that they know your bartenders, most of your other clients, and your staff. They are the ones who know your name when you walk in. Regulars are the ones who come often enough that they pay a good portion of your bills, and fulfilling their desires is a main part of your business. Cultivating and serving regulars, especially long-term ones, are the main goals of most bars. If you go through the effort to create a target market, and all that goes with it, regulars are the ones who will create the profit that you seek.

Having regulars does not mean that you are risk-free; just because you see the same faces week in and week out, does not mean that risk is eliminated. Regulars, who know that they pay your bills, may push for more liberal serving policies than strangers, creating tricky issues to negotiate. As a bar owner, treating all customer the same enforces the notion of fair play; that someone is not getting away with something because they order more. Treating all customers the same is easier on the staff; they do not have to remember who has special privileges. Moreover, from a legal point of view, creating and enforcing consistent policies goes a long way in affirmative defense actions. If you want to reward your regulars, do it in ways that help build their enjoyment of your establishment, rather than increase your legal risks. Some suggestions include mugs with their name, designated bar stools, recognition in a Web page or customer newsletter, or a picture on the wall.

A long-term customer's drinking patterns have recently changed: he is drinking more and becoming more belligerent after a few drinks. As an owner, but also a friend, you are getting concerned that he has crossed the line into alcoholism. What should you do?

Alcoholism is a disease that causes physical and mental changes in a person that can be readily visible to others. Unfortunately, unlike other medical conditions, it is one where the patient needs to be ready to be treated before treatment can be successful. Since most programs are abstinence based, understand that you have lost that person as a customer. Now, it is your job, as a friend, to suggest treatment. If they refuse to listen, then, as a bar owner, you have the right to set and enforce limits such as, "Bob can only have one drink and then must leave." You also have the right to refuse service to anyone, and in some states, if a family member requests it, to stop serving a particular customer at their request.

Finally, there are a few other ways to decrease your legal risks with different types of customers. Create a friendly place, encourage regulars to talk with each other and with strangers. Keeping them engaged keeps them mentally active and less likely to consume drinks out of boredom. Have dress and behavior expectations for your establishment, and enforce them. The more likely you have and promote these policies, the more likely that customers will monitor their own consumption and behave in your bar. You may have to post signs on the walls and on your menus, but making it clear that you want well-behaved customers will go a long way toward patrons being responsible for their own behavior.

CHAPTER 5 MANAGER'S TO-DO CHECK SHEET

- Go back to the Chapter 3 check sheet and match your target market to this chapter's suggestions.

- If you have a bar with any of the groups listed in this chapter, are the suggestions part of your usual operating procedures? If not, fix it.

- Find the phone numbers for a local counseling agency or alcohol-abuse hotline, and post in the bar's phone book for reference.

CHAPTER 6

YOUR ESTABLISHMENT AND RESPONSIBLE ALCOHOL SERVICE

Atmosphere and ambiance are two areas that bar owners can control on a nightly basis. Creating customer-friendly yet legally sound practices includes creating an atmosphere that encourages responsible consumption. This chapter outlines how to change your physical surroundings to encourage responsible consumption.

PHYSICAL ISSUES IN A BAR

Creating a place that is comfortable and perceived as safe for your customers is part of responsible alcohol service. The goal is to have surroundings that make people want to stay without compromising their drinking habits. An upset customer is more likely to feel the effects of alcohol, and a nervous customer will consume more recklessly. Designing the bar does not mean hard seats and sore rumps, but rather building a sense of community within the building. Take a look at the following:

Lighting

Seeing what is going on helps you to monitor customers and their consumption. Dimly lit watering holes may seem quaint, but may be legally challenged. Keeping the lights on will also help limit claims against trips and falls. Aim for a level that allows your staff to see what is going on, yet is dim enough for good ambiance. Make sure that you have lighting directly over the bar that allows your bartenders to make drinks and ring up sales. However, keep those lights on a dimmer so that the lighting level between this area and the main floor does not lead to eyestrain.

Seating

In general, the amount and type of seating needed depends on your target audience. A nightclub bar needs less seating than a hotel bar. Seating may also vary from bar stools in front of the bar to tables and chairs in the perimeter. Tables create issues concerning service: will you have a second server who takes orders and delivers the drinks, or are customers responsible for getting beverages from the bar themselves? Having extra servers means that perimeter customers will receive some direct monitoring and counting of drinks, but a bar owner needs to increase the price of drinks to cover labor involved. Some bar owners compromise by having servers during busy times; during slower times, customers fetch their own drinks. Seating at the bar increases a bartender's ability to count drinks and keep track of what is sold via checks in front of the customer.

Seating should be comfortable yet not so comfortable that after a few drinks the customers wants to go to sleep. Couches and comfortable chairs do create ambiance, but make sure that they match the overall concept and that the price of drinks creates a cozy atmosphere, but not too cozy. Hard stools will help to limit a patron's drinking, but not in a customer-friendly way. Before purchasing replacements, have a series of customers try them out before committing to a purchase. Since you want to keep the customers legally sober when they leave, look for seating that will be comfortable for about one to two hours to minimize the amount of drinks, since men will consume roughly three drinks in that period; women, a little less.

Noise Levels

A noisy bar usually leads to increased drinking on a more reckless level. The higher the ambient noise level, the more likely customers will simply drink instead of interacting with each other. Higher noise levels can also lead to confusion, as drink orders may be misinterpreted. Since noise can come from several sources, manage each area separately.

Some noise is ambient background noise: the ice machine releasing its cubes, a neighboring table's conversation, and the television, for example. The more hard surfaces that you have — wood, tile, ceramic, metal — the more noise will bounce off and increase in level. Aim for conversation-friendly — you can have a conversation without yelling across the table and a server can get an order without any misunderstandings. On an average day, move around the bar and sit in several seats to get a feel for problem areas. In some cases, inexpensive padding on the walls may help absorb noise from customers. You may also consider sound-absorption tiles the next time your ceiling tiles need replacement. When you replace your carpet, aim for a thicker commercial pad. Some of these suggestions may have to wait for a remodeling, but where you can, lower noise with buffers, insulation, and doors.

Other noises come from bands, DJs or jukeboxes. Most sound systems will have a series of volume controls behind the bar; be considerate if someone asks for them to be turned down. Separate controls for each speaker are not usually expensive to install. For bands and DJs, decide what your goal is: are they providing dance music, music to just listen to, or background music within the establishment? For background music, the volume should be low enough so that guests can have conversations without yelling across the table. Dance bands and DJs need to understand that customers will drink with the beat of the music: insist that for every three to four fast songs, they play a slower song for people to catch up. At the end of the evening, around last call, only slower music should be played to help slow the rate of drinking.

Layout

Layout refers to what is in your bar and where customers need to go to do certain things, such as order a drink, go to the restroom, or play pool. Your goal is to keep the drink aisle open; if customers feel that they can get up and order a drink when necessary without undue delay, they are more likely to consume responsibly. On the other hand, if a customer has to fight a crowd to get to and from the bar, they are more likely to insist on several drinks per person from the bartender, as the "hassle/value" factor is skewed. Customers also tend to drink more responsibly if the aisles to the restrooms and the exits are clearly marked and easily managed. "Trapped" customers tend to feel uneasy, which in turn increases the likelihood that they will feel the effects of alcohol sooner than normal. Trapped customers are also more likely to lash out violently toward other guests when they feel provoked — regardless of the amount of alcohol that they have consumed.

Obviously, if the bar still only exists on paper, designing elements to avoid bottlenecks is easier to control. Even if the bar is open, several items can be moved to help even out the flow. Remove any partitions — especially if they are non-load bearing — to keep the room feeling open. Use line ropes to manage where customers need to line up for drinks, and have signs or other cues so they know where to enter and where to exit. Keep booth backs low or see-through so that employees can see the entire area. Make sure that any activities, such as a pool table or dance floor, are not in the middle of the path to the bar; you want these places in the open, but out of the main traffic lanes. If possible, consider building half-walls around them with multiple entrance and exit points so that they are physically separated, yet open for monitoring within the establishment. These half-walls also make a good place to set down drinks, so make sure that a ridge or line exists to prevent spills.

EMOTIONAL ASPECTS

Customers who are drinking want to feel safe and secure; if they sense that something is "wrong," they are not likely to turn into regulars. Relaxed customers drink more responsibly; frightened or tense customers will feel the effects faster.

This emotional component is made up from the décor

including colors, art, neon signs on the wall, plus the layout of the place. Do you have visual clues that help customers with their sense of well-being? Check your front door and ambient lighting levels. On a bright sunny, day do customers feel as if they are entering a dark, forbidding cave? Do they sense that once in the blackness, everyone in the bar can see them, but they can't see anyone? This can be easily resolved by installing overhangs, or awnings, over the front door or by creating a vestibule inside which allows a less harsh transition period. Remember that emotions and altitude affect customers' intoxication levels, so making them comfortable helps with this area.

What are your security levels? Some bars, such as neighborhood bars, may only need the security of 911 predominantly programmed into the bar phone. Other nightclubs may require fully uniformed security personnel moving around the bar, watching out for problems. Check with your regular customers: a presence might be needed to assure customers that they can have fun without worrying.

What sort of overall impression does your staff give? Are they welcoming and friendly or curt and rude? Customers try not to get friendly bartenders in trouble through their behavior, but if they feel that the staff are going out of their way to be nasty to them, then they will not care what they do. Because your staff will behave differently when you are in the building and when you are out, it may be worth sending in secret shoppers to check staff's attitude.

What is the overall ambiance? Have you ever been in a bar where décor, music, and customers did not match? When they match, customers sense that everything is okay and they relax. If they do not match, then something is wrong and they end up leaving. Go back, look at your target customers, and make sure that what you have matches their expectations. If you do not match their needs, you may wish to invest in some simple redecorating to attract your target clientele.

CHAPTER 6 MANAGER'S TO-DO CHECK SHEET

- Review Chapter 3 "Target Market" and the suggestions listed in this chapter. Check to see if they match; if not, fix any problems.

- Spend a day, an evening, and a night checking the lighting, sound, and ambiance of the bar.

CLASSIFIED CASE STUDIES

directly from the experts

- An underage patron can be told they will not be served alcohol (because it is against the law), but are welcome to stay and be served a nonalcoholic beverage. It is always a good policy to identify the designated driver up front. This is made easy by offering free nonalcoholic beverages, for the night, to that person.

- There are simple portable driver's license scanners that display age and whether the ID is invalid.

- No one should be served more than two drinks in an hour. In addition to observing visible signs of impairment, there are portable breathalyzers on the market that can be made available to patrons who are concerned or may need to be made aware of their inebriated state.

- MADD's position is that mandatory seller-server training is the best practice, as those employees need to be proficient and educated for the responsibility of performing their job with professionalism, because they are uniquely positioned at the point of sale and the need to make good judgment decisions, in lieu of over-serving drinks for big tips with disregard for customer well-being. The recommended approaches for managing guests are to make food available and cease serving alcohol at least an hour before driving, express your concern if the person appears impaired, take the keys if possible, and offer to get a cab or call someone.

- MADD does not conduct seller-server training, but advocates for it to be mandatory because it is important to have training and protocol established in order to know what to expect and ways to diffuse situations, to avoid drunk people getting behind the wheel and harming themselves, and others, when it can be prevented.

- There is ample information available to the public, and ongoing awareness campaigns, though most people do not fully understand the laws. Bars are in the business to sell drinks for profit, so there is a conflict. Until cultural attitudes about drinking become more self-responsible, there must be countervailing measures in place for public safety. It would be helpful to include DWI laws and penalties in auto registration and driver's license renewals, and for auto insurance companies to do the same in their mailings.

CHAPTER

7

YOUR OFFERINGS AND RESPONSIBLE BEVERAGE SERVICE

O fferings are what you sell: not only alcoholic beverages but also other items, such as food and activities. Careful management of your offerings will help to create a customer-friendly yet legally responsible bar.

TYPES OF ALCOHOL

Most bars will carry three different types of alcohol: well, call, and top shelf. Well is your base liquor; call is a named brand; and top shelf is the most expensive item in a particular line. Using gin as an example: well is whatever the liquor sales rep has on sale this week, call would be Bombay or Beefeater, and top shelf could be Seagram's or Tanqueray brands. Because of differences in how they are made—ingredients, processing and marketing efforts—the cost per bottle of a well versus a top-shelf product can be great.

Further confusing the issue is that each bar's well-call-top-shelf selections are different. A corner bar that serves primarily beer may have one well gin, two call gins and no top-shelf gins. Contrast that with a high-priced inner-city hotel bar, which may have no well, five to ten calls, and an assortment of rare imported top shelf. Obviously, your selections and what brands appear in which level is going to be based on target market, expected cost per drink, and the channel of distribution for a particular item within your locality.

Regardless of how you set up your bar, the relationship between well, call, and top shelf influences how much your customers will drink. Well drinks are considered cheap and easily drunk, calls are to be consumed more slowly, and top-shelf drinks need to be savored over a long period. Since slowing down consumption is a goal, up-selling customers to calls and top shelf is a great strategy for managing service.

In addition to slowing down the rate of consumption, calls and top-shelf drinks are usually more profitable per drink than well drinks. For example, compare the profit of a well gin and tonic with an up-sold Bombay gin and tonic:

	WELL GIN	BOMBAY GIN
Cost per liter bottle	$10	$15
Amount per drink	1 oz.	1 oz.
Servings per bottle	33	33
Cost per ounce	$0.30	$0.45
Cost per drink	$2.50	$3.00
Profit per drink	$2.20	$2.55
Profit per bottle	$72.60	$84.15
Per bottle difference		$11.55

Since the amount of tonic is the same, it will not affect profit difference. If you sell a bottle of gin a week, then up-selling will net you an additional $600 per year in profit. You will get this profit by giving a customer a drink that they will enjoy, rather than simply something to drink.

To convert customers from well requires some up-selling by the bartender and servers. Normally, if you can get the customer to buy the drink initially, all refills after that will be the same drink. Rarely does a person switch from call back to well, and it is hard to sell someone a call once they have consumed a well, unless that liquor is truly bad. Having your servers up-sell means more tips. Up-selling is as easy as asking a customer for a brand name every time they order a drink. A simple dialogue is below:

> Customer: "I want a gin and tonic."
>
> Bartender: "We have Bombay, Beefeater and Tanqueray. Which do you prefer?"
>
> Customer: "Oh, I'll have the Bombay, thanks for asking."

While the well-call-top-shelf strategy is for liquors and cordials, beer may also be sold in this manner, although the breakdown is usually domestic: specialty/imports or cans, bottles, draft. When selling beer, carry the local favorite domestic brand, but try to up-sell your customers into a specialty beer or an import. Since beer drinkers are unusually loyal to their brew, you may need to price your higher-level beers a bit closer to your domestic brands than your well-call-top-shelf liquor spread. Ask your beer distributor for help during the switchover by supplying table tents, posters, special glasses, and other items to help fuel curiosity. Create a "beer of the month" promotion, using your imports to help nudge customers into tasting them. Your goal is to get them to enjoy the import beer more than the domestic and, hopefully, they will consume it more slowly than the regular beer.

For the can-bottle-draft up-sell, usually mentioning that draft beer is available will do the trick. Draft beer, because of its freshness, will command a higher price than bottled, and customers will usually pay for it without question. Because it is draft, customers will drink it more slowly than a bottle or can. The only places that may have issues with draft beer are those places that cannot support the kegs and lines or because of volume cannot wait to pull a draft. In those operations, up-sell from can to bottle as the premier item.

Wine is another area that can benefit from up-selling. Since there is such a wide variety of wines available, it is not hard for a wine sales representative to match wines to your menu items and create a low, medium, and high level for each item. Print the high-priced option on the menu next to the food item to make ordering wines easy for your customers. Given new technology for saving wine left in bottles, the average restaurant can now serve a wide variety of wines by the glass without worrying that it will go bad. For bars that only carry one or two wines, concentrate on getting something decent with the lowest possible alcohol content.

SIGNATURE COCKTAILS AND AFTER-DINNER DRINKS

Creating signature cocktails—especially ones that have some "snob" appeal—is another way to control consumption. Make these drinks with premium liquors and charge a higher-than normal price for them. Contact your liquor distributor for specialty glasses that can be used to serve them; just make sure that the volume of the glass with the recipe is a reasonable amount to serve. Along with the signature concoctions, use a unique garnish to help drive their appeal. Have your liquor distributor contribute signs and table tents as needed.

Another area to explore, and perhaps one where you can switch people from consumption to savoring, is in the cordials and liqueurs "after-dinner drinks." These drinks will be priced much higher than regular cocktails and sold as a premium item. They will have a higher margin for the operation and an increased tip for the server. Finally, as a stand-alone drink, they will occupy the drinker's attention for a while, as they are designed to be sipped rather than gulped. Mix these top-shelf items with other mixers to create unique cocktails for your operation.

DRINK RECIPES

At the heart of the service issue is how much alcohol you serve to your customers. Creating drink recipes for your operation will control how much goes into a drink. In addition to using recipes to calculate potential BAC levels, their use will also do the following:

- Give you the basis for pricing structures for your drinks.

- Help with the purchase of alcoholic beverages from your distributors: if you pour the same amount for each drink, then forecasting purchases will be easier.

- Make consistent beer keg yields and offer a better determination of which items should stay on tap and which should move to a bottle.

- Give you consistent profits for each type of drink.

- Create customer goodwill with consistent-tasting drinks across shifts and bartenders.

- Help create controls, including dram shop enforcement and financial controls that should help your profitability.

A drink recipe is similar to a food recipe — you simply substitute alcohol for food ingredients. When you create a drink recipe, you specify the glass, alcohol, mixer(s), and garnish for each family of drinks. Fortunately, Atlantic Publishing has a CD-ROM Bartender Guide designed for taverns. As an owner, you simply have to add the glass that you have on hand to the recipes for your servers to use.

SAMPLE DRINK RECIPE

Drink: Margarita – One serving is equal to 1.6 drinks for alcohol-equivalency servings.

Glass: 4 oz Margarita glass

Ingredients:
  Lime Juice
  Coarse Salt
  Ice
  1 oz tequila (100 Proof)
  1 oz sour mix/lime juice
  1 oz triple sec (60 proof)
  Lime circle garnish

Method:
  1. Rim glass with lime juice and salt.

  2. Fill shaker with crushed ice.

  3. Add tequila, sour mix and triple sec. Cover with strainer. Shake until frothy.

  4. Carefully add ice to rimmed glass.

  5. Strain liquid into glass, garnish with lime slice.

One aspect of a drink recipe is careful pouring of the alcohol when making the drink. Allowing "free-pouring," where a bartender simply tips the bottle and lets it run, defeats the purpose of a drink recipe. Whether you use shot glasses, posy pourers, lines etched in glasses, or electronic pour devices, you need strict pour controls. If you allow free-pouring, you will have no idea how much alcohol is being served in one glass, no idea how many drinks were sold out of a bottle, and no way to reconcile your sales with your inventory. Also, different bartenders will free-pour different amounts and the same bartender will find it hard to pour the same amount each time a drink is ordered. Evidence of free-pouring will be used against you if you are sued.

It looked like free-pouring, but it wasn't!

A bar, which focused on serving wines, wanted a pour system that was consistent, easy to use, readily available for bartenders and servers (who poured table wines), and yet looked as if they were free-pouring. Their solution: they took a white wine, a red wine, and sparkling wine glasses; carefully measured out clear vase stones in a liquid measuring cup (for example, 6 oz for red wines); and poured the stones into the respective glasses. They then carefully leveled the stones, filled with lightly tinted water, and stuck a fresh flower in each glass. These vases were strategically placed around the establishment: at the bar, on tables, at the server stations, in clumps of three, looking as if they were a trendy decoration. The key came when someone needed to pour a glass of wine, placing it near the appropriate "decorative" glass; the server could then pour the drink until it was equal to the level of the stones. Voila—perfectly consistent servings.

Calculating how much alcohol is in any drink recipe is based on proof or percentage of alcohol. The higher the proof, the more alcohol is involved, and usually the price from your distributor is generally higher. By keeping all alcohol in a certain place in a bar at a similar proof (for example, well liquors are 100 proof) then you can calculate drink recipes easily.

In general, the following drinks contain half ounce of pure alcohol,

ONE DRINK IS EQUIVALENT TO
12 ounces of beer
or
1 4-oz glass of wine—usually 7–14% alcohol
or
A drink made with $1\frac{1}{4}$ ounces of 80 proof liquor
or
A drink made with 1 ounce of 100 proof liquor

The easy part is if the liquor directly correlates to this chart: for example, when a bottle of beer is usually 12 ounces or an 80 proof rye whiskey, such as Wild Turkey is served straight. Other drinks, such as a Screwdriver (vodka and orange juice), can be manipulated to match the chart.

The chart becomes a problem when glasses and proofs do not exactly match. It is easiest to post the following charts somewhere handy so that your servers can refer to them.

BEER CHART		WINE CHART	
1 Drink = 12 oz Beer		1 Drink = 4 oz Wine	
Ounces	Number of Drinks	Ounces	Number of Drinks
6	0.500	3	0.75
8	0.660	4	1.00
10	0.875	5	1.25
12	1.000	6	1.50
14	1.160	7	1.75
16	1.330	8	2.00
18	1.500		
20	1.660		
24	2.000		

LIQUOR CHART								
	Proof							
Ounces	30	50	60	80	90	100	120	150
0.50	0.150	0.250	0.300	0.400	0.450	0.500	0.600	0.750
0.75	0.225	0.375	0.450	0.600	0.675	0.750	1.000	1.220
1.00	0.300	0.500	0.600	0.800	0.900	1.000	1.200	1.500
1.25	0.375	0.660	0.750	1.000	1.130	1.250	1.500	1.875
1.50	0.450	0.750	0.900	1.200	1.350	1.500	1.800	2.250
1.75	0.500	0.875	1.000	1.400	1.500	1.750	2.000	2.500
2.00	0.600	1.000	1.200	1.600	1.800	2.000	2.400	3.000

NONALCOHOLIC DRINKS

If you are going to run a full-service bar with cocktails, then you have the makings for nonalcoholic drinks. Most cocktails can be made "virgin" without alcohol for those who are underage or do not wish to drink. Even without alcohol, most virgin drinks can be priced near their full-bodied cousins at a higher percentage profit margin per drink.

Another area to explore with nonalcoholic drinks involves the "near" beers and wines on the market. Most major beer manufacturers and wine makers have a low- or nonalcoholic version that tastes similar to regular items. Again, items like this can command a slightly higher margin.

Another issue with nonalcoholic drinks includes pricing for water and sodas. Some bars give away free water and soda to the designated driver, or reduce the price of these drinks in comparison to those with alcohol. Follow this strategy, as designated drivers want to have fun, but not at the expense of their wallet. Pricing water and soda at the same price or higher than alcoholic drinks breaks the price/value relationship and will have the designated driver thinking seriously about having an alcoholic drink, as it would be cheaper. Since you want to encourage responsible consumption, price your water and soda accordingly.

Finally, advertise your alcohol-free selections. Your wine or beer distributor can create table tents and posters. Have them add in any signature virgin drinks that you may have. If you have food, you may be able to add alcohol-free drinks to the food menu on the table. The more you promote these items, the more your sales increase.

FOOD

Selling food is one sure way to help reduce the effects of alcohol on the body. Food slows down the rate that alcohol enters the liver, thus keeping patrons sober longer. If they are eating food, then their rate of consumption will slow as well. Items that slow absorption rates the most include all of the usual bar favorites: those that are high in protein and fat, especially fried items, such as chicken wings, fried cheese appetizers, fried vegetable appetizers, and pizzas. Your goal is to try to sell food to customers in order to slow down their consumption rate. Bars that serve more food than alcohol are usually perceived as being less likely to serve patrons to the point of intoxication.

In most localities, serving food requires an additional license and may require adherence to certain kitchen sanitation codes. If acquiring a food license is not possible, then contact your local health department about the following options:

- Prepackaged foods, such as individual bags of pretzels, long-johns, or cheese sticks, that are sealed by the manufacturer and not opened until the guest consumes them. These items are easily stored, do not spoil, are very cost effective, and can command a high margin.

- Arrange with a neighboring restaurant for delivery to your bar. In exchange for advertising and bartender promotions, they make and deliver food to the customer. Usually this does not require a separate food service license, but you may want to stack up on extra paper plates and napkins. If the customer does not finish the food, they can take it home or dispose of it.

If you sell food, make it available whenever the bar is open. If you need to close the kitchen for a period during the day, have bar munchies available through the bartender.

Selling food also offers the following benefits:

If you sell appetizers from one of the major companies such as McCain, Anchor, Brew City, or Riverside, visit their Web sites for free menus and table tents. If you show that you purchased their items from a wholesaler, they will create small "bar-type" menus featuring six to eight items or single-item table tents. Usually you have to purchase at least two items from them, and they will personalize your menus with your name, address, and phone number. Since you design the menu via the Internet, you can add house specialties, and usually a blurb promoting nonalcoholic drinks. The menus are delivered to your door for free, usually within a week or two.

Increases Profits to Your Bottom Line

When you sell food for more than it costs to buy, you increase your bottom line and help cover your overhead costs. Additionally, depending on your market, you can have a higher margin on your food sales compared to drink sales in your establishment.

Helps You Reach Your Desired Target Markets

Certain groups will want food available. If you offer food during normal lunch and dinner times, your customers are more likely to stay at your bar instead of leaving. Generally, the longer people stay, the hungrier they become. Readily available food will keep them in your place, allowing them to sober up before they leave.

Gives You Marketing Flexibility

Many localities forbid "happy hours," where the price of drinks is lowered to attract customers. However, you can offer a "happy hour" where free or low-cost food is available for your customers.

Celebrate football season

Most bars that cater to men between the ages of twenty-two and forty-five are usually heavy on sports. Football season, with games from Thursday to Monday night, can be a very profitable time for a bar owner, but can also be risky, as more games and more time spent in the bar mean that customers may drink too much. One option is to serve "football"-shaped chicken nuggets with ranch dressing dyed to match the team colors. Five good-sized nuggets with dressing will cost you less than $2 and can be sold to a customer for more than $5. You now have a food item that matches the occasion, the target audience, is easy to make, and is profitable.

Some bars give away free pretzels, peanuts, or popcorn, especially if they do not or cannot hold a food license. At a minimum, these items help to slow down the rate of absorption; it's less than a full meal, but it's better than nothing.

ACTIVITIES WITHIN THE BAR

Offerings also include activities, or things that your customers can do while in your bar. Activities make customers want to visit and increase traffic to your operation. Properly planned, they reduce over-consumption in one of two ways:

1. The activity keeps the customer mentally focused on what they are doing instead of just drinking. Their consumption of alcohol slows and they tend not to get intoxicated (TV-related themes, card games, board games, conversation, video casino games, etc.).

2. The activity keeps both hands busy so that they can only drink when it is not their turn (pool, darts, dancing). This, again, slows consumption as the busier they are doing something, the less likely they are to over imbibe.

Activities can cost money, so to recoup the cost of them, you may wish to charge. Machines, such as darts, jukeboxes, pool tables, video casino, arcade, and pinball machines, can be re-tooled to accept money. Board and card games can be purchased for a nominal amount and replaced as necessary. Theme nights revolving around television events, such as football and "must-see TV," are also virtually free for a bar owner.

Other promotional activities include the following:

- Celebrity nights, especially with a local sport legend, are one option. The celebrity can sign autographs while you have a cover charge. You may have to split the proceeds with your celebrity.

- Contests: Sponsor a dart or pool league, or have poker or euchre nights where the winners get door prizes of a nonalcoholic nature. The contests can span several weeks, increasing your local traffic while decreasing drinking by keeping customers busy. Your pool table or game rental supplier can usually help you find appropriate leagues to join, and your other suppliers are a good source of door prices, such as food, glasses, and posters.

- Celebrate holidays, at least the minor ones. Good celebrations include election days (everyone who votes gets a free appetizer), Arbor Day, beginning of hunting season (specials for hunting widows), and end of season (free meal for the hunter with the largest catch in your area). Check out online calendars from the National Restaurant Association, that show months, weeks and days dedicated to certain items. For example, during June, which is National Dairy Month, feature and decrease the price of milk-based drinks, such as White Russians.

- Toast local celebrities, such as your local elected officials, newscasters, and other legends, by naming cocktails after them. Celebrate their birthday with a special on the corresponding drinks or food.

- Theme parties can be a hit. Decide on the theme first, and match the staff uniforms, food and drink specials, and décor to the theme. Themes can match the season (March Madness), be off-track (Christmas in July or Summer in December), or they can be generic (western, Italian night, casino night). You can pick one or two of the most popular and repeat them every year as needed. After you pick the theme, develop a budget for all needed items. Look for cheap posters and decorations from arts and crafts stores, such as Michael's. Uniforms can be easily updated with a trip to a local discounter, such as Wal-Mart or Kmart, to get seasonal items on sale. Glasses can be ordered in advance from your purveyors, and they can usually supply you with table tents and promotional posters. The best part is that most theme-related materials can be stored and reused repeatedly.

- Host fashion shows or lingerie shows for sale. Make sure that this is legal within your state and that no touching is allowed.

- Have trivia night, karaoke night, Monopoly night, or any other popular game on the same night each week. This is a good candidate for Sunday or Monday night entertainment, as they are the slowest nights of the week.

- Invest in the bar basics: pool table, darts, pinball, arcade, and, if legally permitted, computerized games.

If properly executed, activities can be extremely profitable and help to keep consumption moderate. Look at your target customer and what they would enjoy doing in your bar and offer it to them.

Finally, do not underestimate the value of a bartender who is good at conversing with customers. While it is understandable if the house is packed you might not want them conversing at length, during slower times, servers and bartenders can be great attractions for customers, and their skills also increase their tip dollars.

CHAPTER 7 MANAGER'S TO-DO CHECK SHEET

- Look at your types of well, call and top-shelf drinks — do they match your target market?

- Call in liquor sales reps for suggestions on new selections.

- Do you have up-sell alternatives for all well liquors?

- Do you have a signature cocktail or drink?

- Do you have drink recipes for all of our most popular drinks?

- Do you have recipes with the match drink counts based on the liquor you have?

- Do you have nonalcoholic drinks?

- Get some nonalcoholic drink signs and table tents from distributors.

- If you have food, does it match the suggestions listed in this chapter?

- If you don't have food, call your health inspector for approval to offer pre-packaged items or carry-in.

- Do you have activities that match your target market?

CHAPTER

8

SERVING POLICIES AND RESPONSIBLE BEVERAGE SERVICE

By creating careful policies and training employees on techniques, a bar can reduce their risks with service policies. This area includes how to make drinks, when to serve them, and how to employ some common programs, such as designated drivers. Showing that the bar has these policies in effect and that they have trained and monitored staff that follow them, goes a long way toward reducing risk.

MAKING THE DRINKS

In an earlier chapter, creating drink recipes for your most common cocktails was introduced. Creating recipes is one issue; actually getting the staff to use them is another. As a manager, you need to set up a system so that bartenders will follow the established procedures.

Free-Pour Versus Automated Systems

Ban free-pouring from your operation! At a minimum, enforce the use of jiggers, but quickly replace them with "posy-pourers," and later with computerized dispensers that

work like soda guns. Free-pouring not only leaves you at risk
of a lawsuit, as you really do not know how much alcohol
was in that drink. It also wreaks havoc with your profitability
as liquor is one of your most expensive items. A bartender
attempting to free-pour a 1-ounce whiskey portion may get
only 26 servings out of a bottle instead of the expected 33.
By over-pouring nine drinks, you lose the profit from them
and will have to spend money to purchase another liter more
quickly than expected. If you were expecting $1.25 profit
from that drink, then over-pouring has just cost you $11.25
per bottle, and at a bottle per week, you lose $584.48 per year
that should have been in your pocket. Multiply that by all of
your liquors and suddenly computerized systems seem more
affordable. Free-pouring is also not consistent from drink
to drink and is certainly not consistent from employee to
employee.

Some will say that free-pouring is part of the culture of a
bar and that computerized dispensing turns off customers.
Perhaps, but customers may also enjoy knowing that they can
come to their regular watering hole and have drinks that taste
the same no matter which bartender is working. They may
also appreciate that with a standardized pour, they can drink
a certain number of drinks before their BAC levels go over
the legal limit instead of playing a guessing game of how
long it will be before they are affected.

The bottom line is that you are in business to make money.
Stopping free-pouring is the quickest, fastest, easiest way to
add to your bottom line.

Standardized Glassware

With standardized recipes and pouring, a bar manager should be able to stick to a few sets of standard glasses. With standard glass size and liquor pours, mixers, such as juices and sodas, should be adjusted for taste and volume in the glass. Once a portion is determined, glasses are purchased, resulting in consistent-tasting drinks.

A full-service bar, using 1-ounce portions of alcohol, needs the following glasses:

Shot glass	1 oz
Rocks glass	4 to 6 oz
Sour glass	4 to 6 oz
All purpose	6 to 8 oz
Highball glass	6 to 8 oz
Margarita glass	6 to 8 oz
Martini glass	6 to 8 oz

Different Glassware for Nonalcoholic Drinks

An astute bar owner purchases different glasses and keeps them separated for nonalcoholic drinks, such as sodas, virgin drinks, and water. By using different glasses, minors in possession of the "wrong" glass can be readily identified. Using straws and garnishes will not work, as they can be easily removed or switched. Choose glasses with different colors, heights, textures, or stems to distinguish them from alcoholic drinks.

Pricing Strategies

By keeping the price of sodas and water low, you encourage people who will not be drinking to stay sober, and you keep patrons who do not want to drink from consuming alcohol because it is cheaper.

"Near" beers and wines can be priced at 80 to 90 percent of the price of their full-fledged cousins. Mock-tails, or nonalcoholic cocktails, especially those in oversized glasses with ornate garnishes, can also be priced at almost 90 percent of the cost of their counterparts. Price alcoholic cocktails with no virgin counterparts (for example, martinis) more highly than other drinks in their respective categories.

Specialty or house drinks that you are known for can be priced higher than average drinks in your establishment — if they are what you are noted for, make them pay. For most other drinks, stay within a few dollars, and keep an eye on your well-call-top-shelf ratio: wells and calls should be no more than a dollar per drink different in price. Top-shelf drinks command higher prices, but stick to top shelf that can be priced no more than twice your well drinks.

Finally, price your drinks to prevent intoxication. Look at your target market and their disposable income, and price your drinks so that two drinks per person are seen as reasonable. With cheap pricing, you might draw a cheap crowd, but their drinking will put you at risk. Expensive pricing, where a customer can only afford one drink, leaves you as the "special occasion" spot, which is not good for long-term profitability. Making two drinks affordable and the third a stretch may help to curb over-consumption.

SERVING DRINKS

How the drinks get from the bartender to the customer can also be manipulated by a wise bar owner. Showing that customers are served consistently can help with legal claims.

Use Your Cash Register or Point-of-Sale to Track Drinks

Over the last ten years, point-of-sale computerized registers have dropped in price to become surprisingly affordable. Use this to your advantage. Most systems can be programmed with a wide variety of keys, or touch points, for each classification of drinks that you normally sell. In addition, they can be programmed so that the time the drink was served is printed on the check, which is great for tracking how many drinks each person or table has had. Guest checks should be left on the bar for patrons sitting there and in a spot near the register for customers at tables, or with the server who is waiting on them. Managers can make spot checks and discuss customers who concern them with employees. The times should also serve as a warning for your servers that a person is drinking too fast and possibly may be showing signs of intoxication.

If you are still running an old-fashioned manual cash register, then purchase guest checks (less than ½ cent each), and insist that the servers use them. Mark the drink by person and time served and keep as above. Finally, checks and POS register systems go a long way toward making sure that drinks poured were purchased with cash—one easy way to boost your bottom line without serving extra alcohol.

Stacking

Stacking is where a customer has a drink that they are working on and then orders another one before finishing, or another customer buys them a drink. Prohibit stacking in your bar, as the presence of an additional drink may tempt a customer to consume more or faster. Only allow one drink per person at a time. If a customer orders another drink before the first is done, train your staff to say, "When you finish; you wouldn't want your next one to get stale (or lose its head, or the ice to melt)." Make the server confirm that the next drink will be along when needed, not before. Be careful when serving male/female pairs: men will usually finish before women, and as the alcohol affects the woman faster, do not serve until she is done with the first drink. If one customer orders a drink for another customer, use poker chips or personalized wooden nickels as a placeholder for the drink, and explain to the receiving customer that they can take it at their leisure. If the customer does not want the drink now, or on that day, you may want to consider converting placeholders to gift certificates.

Shots

Shots are certainly tempting and a fast way for customers to get drunk. Whether you call them shots or shooters, they are a risky way to serve alcohol. Consider banning them unless your target market demands them as a matter of course. If you feel you must have them, then:

- Offer only one shot per person per hour.

- If you have roaming shot servers, have only one working the floor, and make sure that they stick to one shot per person per hour.

- Do not let rounds of shots for a celebration to get out of hand, such as multiple shots for a birthday guest of honor. Explain to their friends that the guest of honor needs to make the decision to drink and must order their own.

- Do not start selling shots at opening time, and shut down the sale or ordering of shots a couple of hours before closing.

Pitchers

Pitchers of beer and other drinks are an easy way to serve many people at a table, but watch that you are not sacrificing service convenience for prudent alcohol service. Evaluate the reason why you have pitchers and what you expect to accomplish. Manage pitchers as follows:

- No pitchers at tables with underaged patrons, especially tables with teens or early twenties present.

- Make the price of a pitcher close to the price of the corresponding number of drinks so that a pitcher is not seen as a bargain. For example, if you sell a 16-ounce draft beer for $2.50 and your pitcher holds 64 ounces, then do not price the pitcher below $9 (90 percent of $2.50 times 4). Keeping the price close to that of individual drinks will help to sort out bargain hunters.

- Slow service of alcohol to the table with pitchers: wait until they empty the pitcher before refilling.

- Consider prohibiting pitchers for two-person parties.

- Use smaller pitchers and glasses for each table.

With a pitcher, since you cannot tell who is drinking how much, servers will need time to monitor behavioral changes. Use the same policies for stacking to prohibit multiple pitchers on the table at one time.

Trays

Obviously, trays are handy for your servers; how else will they get a party of ten all of their drinks in one round? Keep trays for your staff's use, but inaccessible to customers. If needed, get four-cup fiber trays, or require that more than one customer comes to the bar for the order. Hiding trays means that customers cannot easily carry multiple drinks and can carry only two at a time, limiting their consumption.

Waiting for the Order

Train your staff to stop by the table to check on service, but to wait until the customer asks for a refill on alcoholic drinks. Waiting until the customer requests a drink will help them monitor their consumption.

Serve Water

Serve water to your customers: aim for one glass per hour per patron. When a customer comes in, give them a glass of water as they sit down for them to drink while taking their order. Water cuts down on the dehydration associated with alcohol and helps to slow its absorption rate.

Slowing Service

If a customer begins to show signs of intoxication, have the server slow service. By slowing service, the server remains in the room monitoring the situation, but is "busy." Some time-honored techniques include the server talking to other tables, bussing tables, serving food or free pretzels, lightly cleaning, or running back to the kitchen to replenish supplies. The perception is that they are too busy to come to the table right away, but will be back in a minute or so to serve the customer. Slowing service keeps the server out of the line of fire without the customer feeling that they have been abandoned or willfully neglected. Once an order for additional drinks has been placed, the server can still slow service by waiting for the bartender, waiting for the keg to be tapped, waiting for additional bottles to arrive from the storeroom, etc. Slowing service is a simple way of keeping a patron from getting intoxicated by allowing time to for their body to metabolize the alcohol.

DEALING WITH CUSTOMERS

Some bars have adopted these common policies as a benefit to their customers. Most of them are low-cost in nature and show law officials that you are serious about responsible service.

Wrist Bands

If you have a mix of legal and close-to-legal-age patrons in your establishment, consider purchasing wristbands for the legal-aged patrons. Banding them upon entrance allows for matching of drinks and glassware to the bands. A server will still have to check IDs at the table, but legal-aged patrons do not usually take bands off for minors to use.

Doormen—Checking IDs

Having a doorman check IDs at the door, under bright lights, is a good policy in some types of bars. While the server is still responsible for double checking before serving a drink, doormen can create a sense that minors and uncontrolled drinking are not allowed. Doormen can also refuse entrance to intoxicated patrons and document that they did so—and call the police if the customer refuses to take a cab.

Designated Drivers

Designated driver (DD) programs, where one person abstains for the evening while the other consume alcohol, has been a bar standby for at least two decades. Promote your designated driver program with table tents and posters, showing food and low-cost drinks, such as soda and water. Some bars will have programs where the DD has a button, pays no cover charge, and has free sodas all evening. For an owner, the cost of sodas is far cheaper than a potential lawsuit. If possible, speak with other bar owners about a community DD program with identifiable hand stamps, so that the DD in "Bar A" does not leave and begin drinking in "Bar B."

Designated driver programs work best for bars that are not serviced by public transportation or a taxi service. If you are a bar owner in that situation, having a DD program will increase your sales, as guests who have DDs will not be afraid to have a drink, as they don't have to drive. If you have a DD program, other guests in the party still need their consumption monitored. You are still legally liable if a drunken guest falls or is hurt getting into a car, even if driven by a sober driver. Finally, if the DD begins drinking, present the group with a check for the sodas that were consumed.

Free Drinks

Freebie promotions have always been a part of this industry, but as far as alcohol is concerned, they need to be monitored carefully. Most localities have banned "two-for-one" and "drinks-as-a-prize" promotions, so this area is carefully regulated. While other uses of free drinks may be legally allowed, use some of the following techniques to regulate them:

- When introducing a new drink, give out 1-ounce portions to the customers as tasters. That is enough for them to get a sense of the taste, but with a miniscule alcohol amount.

- For long-term patrons, consider giving a free meal for major events, or if you do not serve food, give a prize such as a mug or "their" barstool. Avoid giving free drinks as a reward for patronage.

- Give your staff gift certificates to local businesses or for their cable or phone bill instead of drinks at your bar. Consider general traveler's checks, which are good anywhere, for employee of the month, rather than a drink. This does not discriminate against employees who are below legal age and those who do not drink much.

- If you need to give a customer a freebie because of bad

service or a burnt dinner, consider free desserts or a certificate for free appetizers on their next visit. This accomplishes two things: first, it will get them back in again, where you can make the next visit better, and secondly, giving alcohol to an upset or angry person simply makes the effects show faster.

• Employees should not get free drinks. Giving an employee a free drink at the end of the night when they are tired means that the effects will hit them faster. If they want to visit your establishment, then they need to be paying customers.

Cover Charges

Cover charges are designed to bear the cost of entertainment, such as a band, or to restrict access to only those willing to pay. Nominal cover charges do not serve any purpose except to look as if the bar owner needs extra money. Set your cover charge price so that the cover charge plus two drinks is a reasonable sum for your target audience. Make sure that if you have a cover charge, it is enforced later in the evening, including after 11 p.m., and have it for everyone, with no "ladies' night" freebies.

Cab Policies

Find and work with a local cab company for customers who are too intoxicated to drive home. Most cab companies will supply you with table tents and posters. Arrange for one or two cabs to come by every hour if you are in a main traffic area. Most cab companies, in exchange for exclusive rights to pick up at your property, will give you a discount for calls you make and pay the calls on a customer's behalf.

If you are located in a large city, consider petitioning your local tavern league or tourism bureau to support a cab program where cab fares are paid out of a per-drink fund. All bars put in money based on the number of drinks served, and cab rides are paid from this. If an every-weekend program is too cost-prohibitive, then work on a program for your busiest nights of the year, such as New Year's and other high-drinking occasions.

Last Call

Last call, when you tell your customers that you are closing, it can be a legally challenging time to serve alcohol. Make an announcement about one hour before closing time that it is time to think about going. Make last call no later than 30 to 45 minutes before the actual close. Do not serve pitchers, shots, or other high-liquor drinks during the last hour. Turn on the lights, lower the music volume, and begin to assess your customers before they leave. Call cabs at the one-hour mark if necessary. Make sure that no drinks are served after last call and that all patrons have exited the building by closing time.

CHAPTER 8 MANAGER'S TO-DO CHECK SHEET

- Do you still have free-pouring? If yes, buy jiggers, and call your sales representative for a computerized system.

- Do you have different-colored glasses for nonalcoholic drinks? If not, order some.

- Have you reviewed your pricing structure on alcoholic

and nonalcoholic drinks? Fix discrepancies.

• Do you have a POS system or checks in the building?

• Do you have written policies, ready for training on stacking, shots, pitchers, last call, water, free drinks, trays, waiting for order, slowing service, and cover charges?

• Have you talked to a local cab company and received their posters?

• Have you discussed a designated driver program with other local bars?

My name is Elizabeth Gallucci. I supervise the Responsible Alcohol Management Program (RAMP) for the Pennsylvania Liquor Control Board. This certification program is currently the only thing a licensee in Pennsylvania can do to demonstrate that they have taken steps to be a responsible business. It is a voluntary program and was recognized by Pennsylvania legislators in 2001. RAMP has a staff of 11 people that are responsible for approximately 18,000 licensees state-wide.

The key is to have adequate staff on duty. Additional staff in the form of security or who are not serving but are overseeing the patrons' behavior and consumption rate help tremendously. Other things to keep in mind are visual restrictions, including lighting. If you have a doorperson greet each patron, they can look for signs of impairment or a smell of alcohol on them. Servers need to be particularly aware of the patron's condition before service. Waitstaff need to be talking with and evaluating each customer before serving them any alcohol.

Problems that turn into something bigger started as something seemingly trivial. Staff that are well trained and have good communication skills can identify potential problems and address them effectively. Don't serve minors, don't over serve patrons of legal age, and document anything that happens and the actions taken by the licensee.

We would suggest that some type of formal training is beneficial. Dispensing a legal drug is a big responsibility. Owners should have a full understanding of what alcohol does to people as they drink and knowledge of responsible practices to keep their patrons and the community at large safe from alcohol-related incidences.

Liz

The Pennsylvania Liquor Control Board Responsible Alcohol Management Program Certification

Legislation enacted June 18, 2001, established a <u>voluntary</u> Responsible Alcohol Management Program certification that provides incentives for licensees who participate. Completion of the program provides certification for two years. There are five parts to the program:

1. Owner/Manager Training – At least one owner or manager must attend a free training session offered by the Pennsylvania Liquor Control Board (PLCB). These training dates are available online at **www.lcb.state.pa.us**, click Alcohol Education, RAMP, Owner/Manager Trainings.

2. Alcohol Server/Seller Training – At least 50 percent of the licensee's alcohol service employees must complete a server/seller education program conducted by a PLCB-approved independent trainer (this includes anyone who is in the position to serve alcoholic beverages and/or check IDs). Upon completion of the program, employees are required to complete a course examination and must receive an 80% or better.

3. New Employee Orientation – New employee orientation must be provided on or before the first day of the employee's employment as a member of the licensee's alcohol service staff. The Board will provide the licensee with a checklist and appropriate learning methods, and licensees must maintain these records. A definition of a new employee is an individual who has not been employed at the licensed premises in any capacity during the preceding year.

4. Signage – Posting of signs regarding responsible alcohol service. Signage will be provided by the Board; however, the licensee may use other signage provided that it is equivalent in size, number and content to the Board's. Signage must be prominently displayed so that it can be observed readily by patrons. Licensees shall be responsible for posting and maintaining the signage at all times.

Signage shall minimally include the following information:

A.   Acceptable forms of ID.

B.   Refusal of alcohol service to minors and visibly
     intoxicated patrons.

5. Certification Compliance Appointment and Visit – The final component
consists of a compliance visit from your Regional RAMP Representative. After
successful completion of the four above-listed requirements necessary to receive
official PLCB-RAMP Certification, you must contact your Regional RAMP
Representative and arrange a time and date for a visit to your establishment
to review and complete the necessary documentation.

Benefits to the licensee include:

•   Possible reduction in the fines and penalties issued
    by the Administrative Law Judge to the licensee
    for serving a minor or a visibly intoxicated patron, so long as the
    licensee was in compliance with all parts of ACT 141 at the time of the
    violation and had no citations in the previous four years.

•   Knowledgeable, responsible, well-trained alcohol service staff and
    management.

•   Recognition as a responsible licensee in your community.

For more information, check out:
www.lcb.state.pa.us
1-866-275-8237

DON'T DRINK & DRIVE!

Drinking and driving is the number one killer of Americans between the ages of 17–24.

One person is killed in drunk driving accidents every 22 minutes.

The level of legal intoxication is .08 in most states. Several states have additional definitions for people under age 21 (.00-.02). Some states also have mandatory jail time for drinking and driving while intoxicated. Is it worth it?

Don't Risk It!

Cab Company   Phone

Alcohol Awareness & Prevention

© 2005 Atlantic Publishing Group, Inc. • Item #DDD-PS to re-order please call 1-800-814-1132

ALCOHOL AWARENESS POSTER: Don't Drink & Drive
Posters are printed in full color and laminated to reduce wear and tear. It measures 11" x 17". Available from Atlantic Publishing, Item # DDD-PS, $9.95. To order, call 1-800-814-1132 or visit www.atlantic-pub.com.

EMPLOYEES AND RESPONSIBLE BEVERAGE SERVICE

E mployees make or break an alcohol service program. If they do not buy into the actions, then your plans will be carried out reluctantly. With proper motivation and training, employees will be your greatest asset.

WANTED: GOOD BARTENDER

Must be personable and knowledgeable about a wide variety of subjects to talk to our guests. Candidates must be able to remain neutral in terms of local and national politics, religion, and current affairs. Must know how to make a variety of drinks and keep track of all prices. Need to have extensive knowledge of alcohol products, their taste profiles, and be able to match them to customer desires. Must be able to fix dishwasher, jukebox, and toilet. Needs to have at least two hundred songs committed to memory and be an expert on trivia. Must be completely honest, so that they can be entrusted with cash, alcohol, and keys. Must be able to handle difficult situations with aplomb and be able to document all incidents. Need to be reliable and dependable, and available to work on days off if needed. Must be able to carry full cases of bottles and move them from storeroom to bar. Need to know how to clean common bar equipment including blenders, lines, and guns. Must be willing to smile when dealing with difficult customers. Need to be able to offer outstanding service to customers and be innovative in creating drinks and contests for customers. Must have all necessary licenses including sanitation, bartender license, and proof of alcohol-related service training. Must be willing to work for local prevailing wages; tips to be discussed at interview. Must be available to start tomorrow and guarantee not to leave without one month's notice.

Finding a good bartender is hard to do. Finding good servers — employees who sell and deliver drinks to a customer — is a bit easier, but still an issue for most bars. While a good bartender is worth their weight in gold to an owner, the best part is that they make most of their wages from tips. A bad bartender, on the other hand, can cost an owner in lost assets and customers in the long run. While the above description is tongue in cheek, it represents what most bar owners want from a good bartender for their operation.

The first step in finding good bartenders is to write a job description for your establishment. Creating the details of the job will help you to focus on what is necessary. Good bartenders who match your establishment will be happy and accumulate enough tips to make leaving rare.

LEGAL REQUIREMENTS

Most states will have legal requirements for bartenders; check the Appendix for details on your area's requirements. In addition, some local laws supersede state requirements, so check carefully. If you offer food, your bartender may have to take a sanitation course; check with your local health inspector for details.

Regardless of legal minimum ages, older bartenders and servers who are more experienced usually have a better track record with alcohol training comprehension and usage within the establishment. Someone with several years of experience should know how to read customers and be able to detect minors. Experience also means that they have seen most common situations previously and have a sense of what works and what does not. For inexperienced bartenders, not having this track record means when something happens, they may not fully comprehend what is going on and may possibly compromise your training plans.

EDUCATIONAL REQUIREMENTS

Obviously, the more a potential employee knows about bartending in general, the less overall training they need — only what is necessary for your establishment. A good bartender needs to know how to make all of the basic drinks and what alcohol you have to sell. If you have a beer bar, a fine-wine bartender may not be the best fit, unless they are willing to learn about the variety of beers available. Bartenders with a wide variety of experience usually have solid product knowledge, meaning they can match drinks to customers' desires. Finally, they need to know what your best sellers are and what glasses in which the various drinks go.

The second part of general training is knowledge of common bar activities, such as making change, sequencing drink assembly (this drink first, this drink next), cleaning glasses, and bar equipment. Since most bartenders learn these jobs early on, requiring them to demonstrate their skills is reasonable.

Check with your liquor distributors so that you can set up product training. They can come in to teach your staff about what they sell. Beer representatives can explain how beer is made, how to tap a keg, and how to pour. Wine representatives can explain how red and white wines are made and why there are differences in price and tastes. Liquor distributors can explain all of their products. Finally, they can show your staff how to clean the equipment associated with each product line and the importance of correct service. While this does not ensure responsible service, per se, servers who know their products can make intelligent up-sell decisions and better determine customers' needs. They also tend to take a sense of pride in their knowledge and do not want customers to consume to get drunk, but rather to savor the offerings available. Product training is usually inexpensive, as all that the owner pays for is the labor cost for the sessions. Training can be scheduled on a quarterly basis for each group of liquors.

Checking honesty requires checking references and speaking with former employers. Most bartenders tend to stay local, so chances are their last boss may be a competitor of yours. In some instances, your candidate may not wish to inform their current boss that they are leaving, so you may need to go back to a previous employer to check their reference. Bar owners being honest about possible theft and other issues ensures that good bartenders will stay in an area, while the bad ones leave. Do be careful to only ask questions that are legally allowable for references and make sure that you follow guidelines for giving references.

OTHER REQUIREMENTS

Finding potential bartenders who interact well with customers is an important component of responsible beverage service. Employees who are sympathetic to guests are more likely to be perceived as caring for guests, rather than as drill sergeants who bark orders. Drill sergeants are perceived as being inflexible and uncaring, causing arguments and fights rather than offering low-key intervention. Friendlier staff usually equates to more controlled drinking, as customers do not want to get their "friends" in trouble.

Another key component is how well your staff get along with each other. You do not want them so cozy that they can steal from you, but staff that respect each other and are supportive of each other will help each other when dealing with problem customers. When employees are busy fighting, or are so new that they do not know each other, their natural peer support is gone.

STAFFING LEVELS

One area that managers can positively influence to mitigate legal risk is in having adequate staffing levels. Ensuring that an adequate number of employees are working means that staff is able to carefully monitor guests' behavioral changes and can institute service intervention. Having too high of a staffing level in a bar increases labor costs, decreases each individual's tip earnings, and may hinder productivity with extra people bumping into each other. Managers need to take into account monitoring customers when they are staffing the establishments, especially during busy times. An average bartender can usually make 95 drinks in an hour: roughly 50 men drinking 2 drinks an hour, or 80 women drinking 1 drink every 45 minutes. This figure includes time for the bartender to ring tabs, clean glasses, and stock supplies during pauses. Another possible way to schedule bartenders is noting that that every 15 to 20 feet of bar needs its own bartender on busy nights so you can schedule based on floor space. Overcrowding too many bartenders behind the bar may result in trouble, as they will have a hard time maneuvering around each other.

Drink-only servers on the floor can usually handle about 50 patrons an hour; servers with a full-service food menu, about 30 to 35 customers. If your operation serves somewhere in between those numbers, then figure an amount in between. Server loads will be affected by the distance to the bar, the distance to the kitchen, and how long it takes to get a drink. If you are going to be busy, it may make sense to set up another bar in the back-of-the-house for the servers to get their drinks. Pay the bartenders a higher hourly rate to motivate them back there.

Other personnel in the establishment may be added as
needed. Schedule two or three doormen instead of one so that
the crowd cannot rush them and there is bottleneck in case of
trouble. A second set of eyes is also handy when determining
underage or inebriated guests. Bar backs, who keep liquor
stocked and glasses cleaned, can be added on busy nights to
take the pressure off the bartenders. A host may be needed
to seat people and keep an eye on the floor for problems.
Finally, at least one duty manager is needed for dealing with
problems and general overall observance.

TRAINING ISSUES

Training employees needs to be an ongoing venture for most
bars, rather than a once-only event. In addition to normal
training upon hiring, which covers house policies and payroll
paper work, a manager needs to check licensing requirements
and proof of completion of alcohol service training. This
training needs to be ongoing, perhaps with a quick refresher
class scheduled each quarter to review common issues
and problems. Staff who have refresher courses tend to
slow service and start intervention earlier than those who
have only had an initial course. Quarterly training sessions
reinforce the notion that it is important to follow procedures
and maintain logs for each incident. Training also helps
employees to understand their legal responsibilities should
something happen.

Training on a quarterly basis can be expensive, but by using the training programs in Section III of this book, an operation can offer courses on a regular basis. A bar needs to have initial training, perhaps each month, for new hires—or if a seasonal business at the beginning of the season, then quarterly after that. Other options for training include online and via a computer disk that servers check out and return when finished.

A suggested sequence is to work according to the weeks of the month. For example, the first Monday of the month all employees hired in the previous month have their mandatory responsible beverage service training session. On the second Monday of the month, alternate beer, wine, and liquor representatives for product training sessions. On the third Monday at the beginning of each quarter have mandatory quarterly refreshers. On the fourth Monday, repeat whichever session you feel necessary. Keep track of attendance, and pay employees for attending. If they miss a session, then they need to make it up next time. Of course, vacations, scheduled closed times, and holidays may throw the sessions off track, but the occasional fifth Monday should get the system back on schedule. By scheduling training sessions in advance, employees are able to alter their commitments so that they can attend.

LONGEVITY ISSUES

Having long-term staff contributes toward the financial and overall health of an operation in many different ways. Since they usually get some raises over time, their higher pay helps to keep them at your establishment. Long-term employees have a personal or emotional stake in the business and want to see it succeed. They have a good sense of the regulars and areas where your business may be vulnerable in terms of serving alcohol. Long-term employees also have a sense of your business philosophy, whether you have it written down or not, and have worked long enough to know your house policies concerning intervention with intoxicated customers.

Keeping staff over the long haul makes sense financially for reducing risks in serving alcohol. Having short-term employees or a high turnover means that by the time someone has had training in your policies, you need to train someone else. Finding ways to keep employees over the long term goes a long way toward minimizing your risks.

MANAGEMENT SUPPORT

From the employees' point of view, the one criterion for the success of an alcohol management program is management support. If they see managers believe in and enforce training, they are more likely to follow given procedures. If they know that their decision to slow service or cut a customer off will be supported by the manager on duty, instead of being overruled, then they are more likely to follow policies. Managers who make statements about service with no backup are more likely to have meaningless policies than established procedures.

CHAPTER 9 MANAGER'S TO-DO CHECK SHEET

- Do you have job descriptions for all bartenders and

related personnel?

- Check the information in the Appendix and add details to job descriptions as needed.

- Do you have documentation on all the legally required certificates for all of your employees?

- Do you have a written staffing plan; for example, how many people you need to work for each particular level of expected business?

- Do you have a training plan? If not, prepare to write one based on the last section.

- Do you have a training budget?

CHAPTER 10

WHEN BAD THINGS HAPPEN TO GOOD BARS

S ometimes, despite the best of intentions, something happens and your bar falls under investigation. This chapter tells you how to set up paperwork trails and documentation so that if you do run into problems, producing documentation will be the least of your concerns.

FIND A GOOD LOCAL LAWYER

Find a good business lawyer in your area that has a background in alcohol-management issues. Find the lawyer ahead of time and put them on retainer to review your documents and other necessary items. Fellow local hospitality managers and your local bar association should all be good sources for candidates. After you have the documentation section finished, have them review it for local suitability.

CREATE YOUR RESPONSIBLE BEVERAGE SERVICE POLICY

Use this book and the corresponding CD-ROM to create a hard copy of your policies. Include information that is unique to your establishment and print away. Make any changes suggested by your legal advisor. Put the date of issue on the cover so that you can make sure that everyone has the latest version.

When finished, one copy remains in the building and one copy outside the building, perhaps at your house. Every employee should receive a copy and sign that they have read and will follow the document. All new employees should also receive and sign for a copy. Include a passage that states that if they do not follow the written policies, they may be terminated. Final copies should be kept with your lawyer and filed with your local alcohol licensing board.

KNOW YOUR CIVIL OFFICIALS

Get to know your local chief of police, sheriff, and alcohol commissioner. Join the chamber of commerce, local tavern league, local restaurant association, or some other popular civic-minded group. If local officials have a good and favorable impression of you and feel that you are a responsible server of alcohol, your reputation will grow within the community.

Also, get to know and become a patron of your local MADD chapter. Stressing that you want to serve alcohol in a way that is sensitive to their concerns will help your reputation as a responsible bar.

Finally, make an effort to establish a connection with local churches, especially of those faiths that are anti-alcohol. Make donations from your business, rather than trade name, to their local charities. Even just donating water for special events can be helpful in establishing your reputation as a respectable businessperson.

In short, socializing does your business good, especially if local bars do not have a good reputation to begin with. While some members will not be particularly friendly toward you because of what you own, creating connections will help you establish and keep a reputation as a clean, good-time place.

LOGS

If something happens, the police and courts will look to contemporary evidence: items that were written down or photographed on the day of the problem rather than a few weeks later. Create your logs so that they are part of your daily financial documentation and so that people will remember to fill them out.

Most bars have some sort of daily sales report that calculates the day's receipts and money tipped out. Have every bartender on duty sign off on the back with the date, time, and details of any problems or issues. If nothing happened, have them sign off with a note saying that. A simple "see problem book" notation will direct legal authorities in the right direction.

"Problem log books" do not have to be elaborate: a simple composition book readily available from an office supply store will do. What it does need to have is bound pages so that if a page is ripped or cut out, it will be readily apparent. If an incident happens, have the server or bartender write:

- The date.

- Time.

- Place in establishment — table number, bar stool.

- Description of customer(s) involved.

- What happened.

- Staff involved.

- Other customers involved.

- If they had something to drink, include a printout of their check or a copy of a manual check. Circle in red on the journal tape their last financial transaction.

- Copy of credit card receipt, if used.

- Car license number.

All staff that witnessed the event, or participated in it, need to sign the logbook as well. If you have multiple bars or doormen, they should also have their own logs for practical issues.

TYPES OF INCIDENTS

Log the following incidents:

- Refusal of entrance of inebriated persons.

- Shutting off service of an intoxicated guest.

- Confiscating an illegal ID.

- Shutting off a guest when you discovered they were a minor after they had a drink.

- Fights or loud arguments.

- Trips, falls, or other physical problems with guests.

- Use of a weapon.

- Catching anyone with illegal drugs.

In addition, anything along the lines of a fire alarm being set off, attempted robbery, or a visit from an ambulance should be documented.

DOCUMENTATION NEEDED

You should have a personnel file for every employee, with the following documentation:

- A copy of any state-issued license or certificate they hold.

- A signature sheet showing they received a copy of the responsible beverage service document, have read it, and will follow it.

- A sheet noting date and topics of all training sessions this person has attended, especially off-site state-mandated programs.

You should also have a separate file for training sessions held that dealt with alcohol. Each session should have a sheet with the day, date, participants, lead presenter and their affiliation, any assistants, where it was held, and a one-page summary of what was covered. Have the presenter sign it, and staple a copy of any printed material from the session to the control sheet.

If you take advantage of Internet-based training programs, get a copy of the time logs from the main computer program that runs the training. You want documentation that shows someone looked at this material on certain dates and times. Make sure that the program is interactive and some sort of keystroke capture rate is maintained. Finally, make sure that the time spent is reasonable. You may wish to have this type of training on-site so that you can monitor who does it and how long it takes.

EMERGENCIES

In the event of an emergency, call the local authorities. Program 911 into the phone system so only one key is used to dial. Make sure that you have a landline and cell phone available for staff use while you are open.

As soon as the local authorities arrive, have your staff cooperate with them. Keeping the police away from them will not help you in the end. Unless members of your staff need immediate medical attention, or have been taken into custody by the police, have everyone document what happened in the "problem log book." Do this before they leave and begin to forget or embellish details. Refer authorities to your lawyer.

AFTER THE FACT

One morning as you are opening, local law officials stop by with news of an incident that happened to a possible customer of your bar last evening. As part of the investigation, especially if a breathalyzer test showed alcohol or intoxication, they are interviewing all the bars that the person visited. At this point, especially if you have not looked at the logs yet, request that the interview take place with your lawyer present. Legally, you may be entitled to some basic information, including the name(s) of the victim(s), and the details of what happened.

After they leave, you need to call your lawyer and follow their advice. However, one warning: if in the course of the investigation you discover that one of your employees did not follow your written policies, then that person needs to be terminated immediately to help mitigate your legal liability.

CHAPTER 10 MANAGER'S TO-DO CHECK SHEET

- You have a lawyer that is familiar with local liquor codes.

- You have made plans to meet your local civil officials.

- You have purchased log books and have them in the building.

- You have the Daily Sales Report being signed by the bartenders and other staff.

- You have taken the materials from Chapters 5 through 10, as needed, and printed them out to create your responsible beverage service guide.

- The guide has been edited for your establishment and reviewed by your attorney.

- You have given a copy to all of your employees and have a signed sheet from them saying that they have read it and will comply.

- You have a folder for each employee with all necessary documentation in it.

TM

For over 20 years SADD has been the premier youth-based education and prevention organization addressing serious youth issues, including underage drinking. Research has shown that there are numerous mental, behavioral and health risks associated with underage drinking. Alcohol affects a young person's critical thinking and decision-making skills; increases the risk of violent, anti-social and risk-taking behaviors; and increases the likelihood of alcohol dependency and alcohol-related health problems. One of the most visible potential consequences of underage drinking is impaired driving and alcohol-related crashes, claiming the lives of thousands of young people each year.

SADD is represented in each of the 50 states by more than 10,000 chapters dedicated to educating their peers, parents and community members about the dangers associated with underage drinking. Chapters promote SADD's "No Use" position and do not believe that it is possible to break the law responsibly. SADD and its chapters do not condone or support activities that encourage or enable the use of alcohol by underage people, including designated driver programs for underage people, safe rides programs, parties where alcohol is served under the supervision of or with the knowledge or consent of parents or other adults, or drinking subject to passing a breathalyzer test.

SADD chapters believe in tightening and enforcing the law regarding service to underage drinkers and frequently work with law enforcement through national and statewide campaigns to do that. Many SADD chapters work with licensed beverage outlets in their communities to reinforce enforcement efforts and will commend establishments that follow the law.

Kristin French
SADD

THE TRAINING
PROGRAM

WHO NEEDS TO READ THIS SECTION?

This section of the book works with the information that you gathered in the first two sections, alongside information in the Appendix to create a custom training plan for your establishment. To use, read Chapter 11, which details how to set up the plan, followed by chapters with the actual plans. The goal of this section is to tie your management changes from the previous sections to operational policies, giving your staff guidelines on how to handle most situations.

After preparing your basic training guide, seek local legal counsel to review the sections pertaining to laws in your city or county, especially if the Appendix indicates that local government dictates some operational aspects.

CHAPTER

11

CUSTOMIZING YOUR PLAN FOR YOUR ESTABLISHMENT

This chapter covers some of the logistic issues associated with training plans and sets up the program that follows in the proceeding modules. This part deals with the, who, what, when, and how of training, along with guidelines for using the scripts.

WHO NEEDS TRAINING?

The people who need training in your establishment may be dictated by law. Check the Appendix for information on your state's guidelines about who must be trained in your jurisdiction. Usually, the following people need training in a typical bar or restaurant situation.

Managers and Supervisors

All managers and supervisors who oversee the sale of alcohol need to be trained. Management training should include basic server training and supplemental training on issues related to your establishment, including the policy changes made in the first two sections.

Bartenders

All bartenders who make drinks should be trained. Bartender training should include all of the modules. Stress the use of drink recipes and standardized pouring to this group of employees, as they are the ones who will use them. Bartenders who work service bars also need this training, as they should be able to catch re-orders and notify servers of their concerns.

Waitstaff and Servers

Even though they do not make drinks, this group (after bartenders) does the most serving. They need ID training, training in identifying intoxicated guests, green-yellow-red training, and training in bar policies. This will probably be the largest group of employees, and their training can be combined with that of bartenders and other groups.

Doormen

While they do not make or serve drinks, doormen need, at a minimum, ID training and identifying intoxicated guests training. This group is your first defense against admitting intoxicated customers, and the importance of their job needs to be emphasized. It may be a good idea to combine doormen with servers in training so that both groups can understand how they interrelate.

Valet Parking Attendants

If you offer valet parking and the employees are on your payroll, then they should be trained similarly to doormen. This group offers your last chance to stop intoxicated patrons from driving, and they need to understand the consequences of not allowing them to drive. If your valet parking is provided by another business, work with the owners to have them trained with your staff.

Security Personnel

If you have security personnel working the bar, either in uniform or "under cover," they also need training in identifying IDs and intoxication. Again, if you use a third party to cover this job category, have them trained in your establishment's policies. It will create confusion if your employees are trained one way and your security personnel have different training while working in your establishment. Customers can sense when rule enforcement is different depending upon with whom they are dealing and will attempt to get service from the most lenient member of staff.

If you hire off-duty police personnel for your establishment, hopefully they have had training in the specifics of alcohol service, including identifying minors and intoxication. What they may need is training on how to run interventions within a customer service establishment: an on-duty officer and a waiter dealing with an underage drinker may have the same goal, yet because of training, go about achieving it differently. Ensuring that your personnel have a customer-friendly attitude may mean investing in training on that topic.

Other Employees

A larger bar or restaurant will have other employees involved in the operation. Whether or not they participate in a training program depends on their job description and their normal customer interaction. Some staff, such as bookkeepers, cleaning staff, kitchen personnel, stockers, and other personnel who work when the bar is closed, may not need training.

Personnel such as hosts, maitre d's, cashiers, restroom attendants and bussers, bar backs, coat check, banquet servers, and entertainment personnel may need training in this area. To decide whether they do, look at their job description and observe them during a normal shift. Factors include:

- Are they the first or one of the first employees to see a customer?

- Do they interact directly with customers by clearing tables or bringing appetizers, meaning that they can observe changes in behavior by the guests?

- If they only see a customer once (such as a restroom attendant), is it for enough time to assess intoxication levels?

- Are they one of the final employees that the customer sees?

If you can answer yes to two or more questions for a particular job description, then that position may warrant training in one or more areas. For this group, identifying intoxication may be the best session for them.

WHERE TO TRAIN?

Finding a place to train is always an issue. Your bar may

be an option if there is a time during the week when most employees are available, as it is somewhere that training can go on undisturbed. Training in your establishment has the added advantage that you can walk employees through the actual problem areas, and they will become comfortable with role-play sessions where they actually work. Another advantage is that you can control access to the space. You will also have easy access to all needed materials, such as your glasses, cash register or POS, and pour systems.

The disadvantage of training in-house is distraction from on-duty employees and customers. Employees may also see doing in-house training as another "job," not to be taken seriously. You also risk employees discussing other topics not on the schedule during the session.

Training elsewhere has advantages. If you require employees to travel to another location, they may take the training more seriously. Depending upon where you have the training, educational support materials such as overhead machines, laptops with presentation programs, and microphones may be readily available. The room may also be set up classroom style to emphasize the seriousness of the situation. Finally, out of the building you can restrict potential distractions.

Training out-of-house does have a few drawbacks. Rental charges for hotels and conference centers can be prohibitive. You may need to work with your POS sales rep for a "dummy" or mockup of your system for training purposes. You also need to lug all of the necessary items back and forth.

Some lower-cost options for out-of-house training include:

- Church halls (additional benefit of showing you are a responsible owner).

- Union halls.

- Movie theaters during the day.

- College campuses, especially during breaks.

- Restaurants with a "shower" room that can be closed off from the main dining area.

- Social halls, such as the VFW or Moose Lodges.

Most of these options offer reasonable prices for room rentals, especially during the week, if you book several sessions at one time. Most of them can arrange tables and chairs to your specification and may be able to give you a locked area to store your regular supplies for class.

WHEN TO TRAIN

With the potentially crazy hours in this industry, finding a time to train may be an issue. Day employees may work from 10 a.m. to about 7 p.m., while evening employees, who leave at 3 a.m., may not even wake up until late afternoon. If you are regularly closed one day a week, scheduling training sessions on this day may be your only option, but you risk burnout from staff if they cannot get a full day away from the bar. The second option is to run two classes per day — one in the morning for the early birds or those still awake, and a second class later on for those who did not make the first. This will increase your training costs, and a good trainer needs to make sure that both groups stay on schedule with the topics.

Deciding when to train also includes how often to train on the topics. Going back to previous chapters on training, employees should have an initial training within 30 days of being hired. Refresher courses on various topics should be offered on a quarterly basis, as discussed in earlier chapters.

Communicating with employees, especially when attempting to keep them focused on the issues, may be difficult. Employee newsletters, Web access, or a private newsgroup, such as Yahoo!, may offer a means by which you can send information and post "spot quizzes." Employees with correct answers can win a small prize, or have their name placed in a drawing for a larger quarterly prize during the training sessions. It may also be a way to keep employees interested and up to date on issues concerning the bar.

HOW ADULTS LEARN

Remember the days when school seemed so boring? Make sure that your training sessions are not seen as such. Adults learn best when:

- Sessions are short with breaks.

- They are fed, served water, and have visited the restrooms.

- Each session focuses on one topic.

- They have a chance to ask questions, especially for clarification on what you have shown them.

- They can show their acquired knowledge: they can demonstrate with role-playing or quizzes that they learned the material.

- In the days following the session, management takes special care to focus on the training and reinforcing the objectives.

A module lasts one to two hours: several modules with breaks between them can take a full day. Do not be tempted to run a course for several hours in a row without breaks; too much information means that none will be processed, especially from topics at the beginning. By giving employees a break every hour or after a topic, they can reset their brains and retain what they have learned. Breaks also give them a chance to stretch, move around, and attend to bodily needs that, if not taken care of, may distract them from the material. Employees tend to remember material better when they take an active role in training through scripts, role-playing and questions and answers, rather than sitting and passively listening to materials.

A module is a session devoted to one topic only, and information is self-contained, although topics may build on each other. A string of modules can make up a training program. This program is module-based and the modules are as follows:

1. Legal

2. Medical

3. Red-Yellow-Green system

Each module is designed to stand alone as a topic for a session. The modules can also be mixed and matched; for example, bartenders need to attend all of them, while a doorman may only need sessions one and four. Modules may also be taken out of order, so an employee who needs to miss a session will not be behind in the next session, although all three sessions are necessary. Finally, modules are self-contained, with all information needed within the class.

PROFESSIONAL TRAINER

Do you need to hire a trainer? It is possible that although you are a fantastic bar owner, the thought of leading a training session and delivering lectures is nerve racking. If the thought of this terrifies you, you may want to hire someone to deliver the material. If you want the training program that you have developed but do not want to do the actual sessions, look for a local teacher. High schools, community colleges, religious education courses, and trade unions may all have talented people who can work with the material to present it to your employees. You still need to be present, as only you should answer questions specifically related to your bar. Just make sure that whomever you hire to do the delivery has bar experience and takes a trip through your establishment to see what the employees will be referencing.

MANAGEMENT SUPPORT

The best way to make sure any program succeeds is to support it in the weeks immediately following the session. After learning a new way of doing something, employees are usually enthusiastic about it the next week. As you see or catch someone doing things right, make a point of visibly praising them in front of others; this shows management support and endorsement of training and is a visible reward for learning.

By not supporting training in the following weeks, you risk "business as usual" and a sense that training sessions are merely additional work hours. While this may be tempting — don't. Remember your goal: A customer-friendly yet legally responsible bar. By cheating on the delivery of the material, you leave yourself legally vulnerable, as it is the actual performance of your employees that counts, not the theory.

MODULE FORMAT

Each of the following modules is set up in a similar fashion. First is the manager's to-do sheet, with detailed information needed for that section, specific to your bar. The module itself will start immediately below that. Then to follow will be the unit objectives — what they will learn followed by the body of the section. Icons, as explained below, indicate if a trainer is suppose to be speaking, performing an action, or having the class fill in information. After the main body of the material, there is a recap session, reviewing what has been covered. Next, an assessment, or a quiz, is provided to make sure that students understand what was covered. Finally, answers are included for both the body content and the quizzes presented.

PERSONALIZATION

Gather the materials from the previous chapters and have them ready. The master checklist is below.

- Information for your state from the Appendix.

- Copy of your state's of age and underaged driver's license to show the class.

- Samples of other local identification, such as from grocery stores, insurance cards, or a sample credit card.

- If you are a dram shop state: information on current fines and jail time for violations from your state's liquor commission.

- House policies regarding minors:

  - Do you admit them (restaurant)?

  - How do you identify them?

  - What are your armband and drink glasses policies?

- Cab company(s) phone number.

- Copies of BAC charts from Chapter 1.

- From Chapter 1, your drink count charts, and from Chapter 7, your drink recipes. Make sure that your drink recipes reflect the BAC count.

- Suggestions for service from Chapter 4.

- Have your food menus ready to hand out. Make a list of items that are high in fat and protein, such as chicken strips and fried appetizers, that will help slow the effects of alcohol.

- If you do not serve food, have your list of outside companies that will deliver food to your establishment for servers to hand out.

- If you do not serve food but can sell pre-packaged items, have them in-house and ready to go.

- A list of the alcoholic products that you serve, their proofs, and the average serving sizes for beers and wines.

- A list of suggested up-selling alternatives for all well liquors.

- A premium beer promotional setup.

- Signs and table tents for your signature cocktail.

- Drink recipes for all of your most popular drinks with the applicable drink equivalence count and assigned glass.

- A list of nonalcoholic drinks available and printed on table tents.

- Posy-pourers installed and automatic system on order.

- Different-colored glasses for nonalcoholic drinks.

- Written policies on stacking, shots, pitchers, last call, water, free drinks, trays, waiting for orders, and slowing service.

ICONS

To make the training scripts easier to understand, look for the following icons in each session. The icons are points in the script where the trainer or the class needs to do something or fill in information. Before starting a session, go through the manager's to-do list and insert information in the correct places within the module so that you have one complete copy of each session.

As you go through the session, material will be presented between brackets <such as this>. Anything between the two brackets is for the presenter to use, either giving directions on what to do or showing where information from a manager's check sheet needs to be included. In some cases, the brackets are for the staff to fill in information.

The icons are as follows:

Speaking: The trainer needs to say this material aloud to the participants.

Instructions: At this point in the session, a trainer may need to skip a section depending on their state laws.

To-Do: At this point in a section, the trainer and the participants will be doing something. To-do includes filling in information, acting out situations, or explaining house policies. For to-dos that are written, the information between < and > gives specific details for that answer. For example, the line:

Our state BAC is <fill in from the Appendix >

means that the specific information is in the Appendix, and you need to have it before the training session starts. When you are leading a session, the participants need to fill in this information. They can use pen and paper, or you can copy the appropriate pages to hand out.

Demonstrate: The trainer or participants needs to demonstrate a particular task.

QUICK REFERENCE GUIDE

 **SPEAKING**

 **INFORMATION**

 **TO-DO**

 **DEMONSTRATE**

Scott Young is founder, president and head instructor of **www.extremebartending.com**. The company began in Vancouver, Canada, in January 1994 and is now the most complete and busiest bartending Web site in the world. As creator of the EXTREME BARTENDING™ concept and method, Scott has produced and directed three one-hour volumes, which were released for distribution in November 1998. At that time he also released a two-hour COMPETITION HIGHLIGHTS video. This training series was rated by Nightclub & Bar Magazine as "easily the most complete program available." Scott has written a comprehensive yet entertaining book, *EXTREME BARTENDING™ - SERVE IT WITH STYLE!,* which is pending publication.

It is incredibly difficult to keep track of what everyone is drinking. Realistically, a bartender can only really "keep track" of the people he or she serves, as there are so many people in most bars. Even doing that is often a losing battle, as patrons often go from bar to bar, so a server may only serve them once. It's imperative to pay close attention to the people you serve for the telltale signs of intoxication and take steps if needed.

The best way to identify a problem before it gets bigger is to have the bar staff consciously make an effort to scan the crowd for potential problems and then to step in and tone things down if necessary. Intoxicated people who cause problems don't get that way in five minutes; they get there gradually over time, and if your staff is alert and experienced, they can stop most problems before they get out of hand. I've had great success by being pre-emptive and enlisting the help of the intoxicated person's friends, if they have any, who can handle them easier than a stranger can. If that doesn't work, then you can always step in yourself or have a security person or manager have a talk with them or ask them to leave if it gets to that point.

Many states and provinces are beginning to take this subject seriously and have a mandatory responsible service of alcohol program for anyone who serves it. For places where it isn't mandatory, more and more bar owners are looking for programs and encouraging or demanding that all their employees have some type of training on this subject. Statistics are scary in North America when it comes to drinking and driving accidents, and if the deaths and injuries don't convince the bar owner and managers that proper training is needed, then maybe the bottom line of the large dollar cost of a potential lawsuit will. I consistently get many questions from my

students, working bartenders from all over the world, who know very little about how alcohol affects the human body. I ask the question to every class I teach: "What helps sober your up?" It's very scary to me that many of my students answer coffee, water, salt, hot soup, pineapple juice, etc. Those are real answers. Time is the only thing that will sober you up. Your liver needs time to process and get rid of alcohol.

HOW TO CUT SOMEONE OFF

- Notify manager and/or coworkers.

- Always have a witness present.

- Communicate with guest in private to reduce embarrassment.

- Maintain a calm, courteous, firm approach.

- Listen and empathize.

- Don't back down.

- Explain "Nothing personal, it's house policy."

I recommend that the server always blame it on the manager. Create a house policy that the manager always backs up the server who makes the decision and let the manager take the blame. The server will have an easier time keeping the person calm if the patron thinks the server is on their side but the "big, bad manager won't let me serve you. I wish I could buddy, but I could lose my job. Can I get you a coffee or a pop?"

Do whatever you can to decrease the odds of something bad happening.

The following is directly from our company manual:

ALCOHOL AWARENESS – WHAT CAN YOU DO?

- SUGGEST THAT THE PATRON LEAVE HIS/HER CAR KEYS WITH THE MANAGER, WHO WILL ENSURE THAT THE CAR IS NOT TOWED AWAY.

- OFFER TO CALL A CAB.

- OFFER TO CALL A FRIEND OR RELATIVE WHO WILL AGREE TO DRIVE THE CUSTOMER HOME.

- ENCOURAGE SOBER FRIENDS TO DRIVE THE GUEST HOME.

- PROMOTE A DESIGNATED DRIVER PROGRAM.

- INSTALL A TAXI PHONE AND/OR HAVE PARKING STALLS RESERVED OUTSIDE THE MAIN DOOR FOR THEM.

- PROMOTE THE SAFE RIDE PROGRAM OFFERED IN YOUR CITY OR START YOUR OWN.

- ENCOURAGE STAFF AWARENESS.

IF THE PATRON REFUSES ALL OF THE ABOVE SUGGESTIONS AND STILL INSISTS THAT HE/SHE IS NOT TOO INTOXICATED TO DRIVE HOME, INFORM YOUR MANAGER OF THE EFFORTS YOU HAVE MADE TO PROVIDE ALTERNATIVE TRANSPORTATION.

MODULE

1

LEGAL ISSUES SURROUNDING SERVING ALCOHOL

INTRODUCTION FOR MANAGERS/OWNERS/ TRAINERS

This module introduces the concept of legal responsibility for serving alcohol. This section explains to servers, bartenders, and other employees why they need to "buy in" to the program. Information that you need to collect before you teach this module includes the following:

- Information for your state from the Appendix.

- A copy of your state's of age and underaged driver's license to show to the class.

- A sampling of other local identifications, such as from grocery stores, insurance cards, or a sample credit card.

- If you are a dram shop state: information on current fines and jail time for violations from your state's liquor commission.

- House policies regarding minors:

  – Do you admit them (restaurant)?

  – How do you identify them?

  – What are your armband and drink glass policies?

- Cab company(s) phone number.

Have this information ready to present at the training session. The students will retain the information more easily if they write it down, but having it on hand will make things simpler for you.

LEGAL ISSUES – TRAINING MODULE

 ## MODULE OBJECTIVES, OR WHY DO I NEED TO WORRY ABOUT THIS?

- If you serve a minor, you may be fined and fired.

- If you keep serving someone who is intoxicated and they injure someone, you could be sued and/or fined and/or face criminal charges.

- If you are fined, then you must pay the fine. This company cannot legally pay your fines or reimburse you for them.

- If you violate state laws, there is a possibility that you may not be able to bartend or serve again in this area.

- Even doormen and valets have been held liable for allowing in intoxicated people or minors and have been held liable for allowing intoxicated people to drive.

- Laws have been passed that possibly make you more responsible for a guest's consumption than the guest.

WHAT IS THE PURPOSE OF THIS TRAINING?

This training session focuses on our policies concerning serving alcohol. It also shows you how we want you to handle difficult situations. With this training, you may not be liable if something happens if you follow our instructions. This training is to help all of us respond to customers in the same way and to solve problems the same way each time.

 <Note to Managers: Dram shop states continue here, common law states skip to the similar section below>

DRAM SHOP LAWS

We are in a dram shop state, which means in our state:

- It is illegal to serve someone who is a minor (under 21).

- It is illegal to serve someone who is intoxicated.

 If we serve anyone in those two groups, we face:

<circle>

Fines
Jail Time
Being Sued
All of the Above

Fines can range from $ <fill in> to <fill in with state information>

Jail time can range from <fill in> to <fill in with state information>

Third parties can sue both the bar and the server. Who is a third party? If you serve Tom beyond his legal limit and Tom then causes a car accident, killing Tony, then Janna, Tony's wife, can sue you. Janna can sue you for all costs including medical, burial, loss of income, loss of companionship, damage to the vehicle, and any other economic loss that she may have suffered. Janna can sue both the bar and you, the server.

 <Note to dram shop state managers: Skip to "Other Laws in Our State" section, common law states start here>

COMMON LAW STATES

We are in a common law state, which means in our state:

- It is illegal to serve a minor (under 21).

- If we serve someone who is intoxicated, then we may be sued if they cause an injury. If a reasonable person could see that the person was so intoxicated that they should not have driven, then we may be held liable (legally responsible).

In our state, third parties may be able to sue the bar and the server. Who is a third party? If you serve Tom so many drinks that he is obviously intoxicated when he leaves, and then Tom causes an accident that kills Tony, then Janna, Tony's wife, may be able to sue. She can sue for any economic costs associated with Tony's death if the lawsuit is successful.

OTHER LAWS

Other laws in our area based on our license that you need to follow:

<Have the participants fill in the information>

We can serve alcohol from: <fill in> time to <fill in> time on the following days: <fill in>

To pour a drink, a server needs to be <fill in> years old.

To serve a drink, a server needs to be <fill in> years old.

We need to have signs posted on <list topics>.

Our house policies include:

Minors: <circle the option>

We let them in.

Minors are not allowed in at all.

If we let minors in, they need to <fill in information on where in the building, time of day, identification, etc.>.

We have a wristband policy: <fill in with details>.

We have a policy on glasses just for nonalcoholic drinks <fill in with details>.

IDENTIFYING MINORS

In our state, only the following IDs are acceptable: <list>

FIGURING OUT WHO IS A MINOR

Only people who are 21 years old or older may legally drink. To figure out if someone is legal, then look at their ID and calculate their age.

1. Subtract 21 from this year.

    Example: 2006 – 21 = 1985

2. Anyone born before this year is legal; anyone born after this year is not.

    Example: Anyone born before 1983 is legal; anyone born in 1985 and after is not.

3. Anyone born this year needs another calculation.

    Example: Anyone with a birth year of 1984 will need another check.

4. Look at the birthday and compare to today.

    a. If the birthday is today or before today, they are legal.

b. If the birthday is after today, then they are still a minor.

<Read the example and walk through how to calculate.>

Examples:

1. Today is September 1, 2005. Jane's birthday is May 15, 1982. Is she legal?

   Answer: Yes: 2005 – 21 = 1984; since she was born in 1982, she is legal.

2. Today is June 15, 2006. Ethan's birthday is October 24, 1986. Is he legal?

   Answer: No: 2006 – 21 = 1985; he was born after, so he is not legal.

3. Today is October 30, 2005. Amy's birthday is August 8, 1984. Is she legal?

   Answer: Yes: 2005 – 21 = 1984. Since her birth year is 1984, then she needs a further check.

   August 8 is before October 30, so she is legal.

4. Today is February 22, 2006. Ben's birthday is July 26, 1985. Is he legal?

   Answer: No: 2006 – 21 = 1985. Since that is his birth

year, then you need to compare dates.

February 22 is before July 26, so he is not legal.

IN-CLASS TO-DO

<Have the class do the following examples on their own; check answers.>

Today is March 17, 2007. Are the following customers legal?

Chuck   12/7/42

Jimmy   1/4/87

Brian   2/10/86

Barb   5/8/70

Anne   9/3/90

Mike   10/6/86

Tony   1/23/85

Pam   10/14/83

HOW TO CHECK THAT IT IS A VALID ID

<Show the participants the actual ID that you have borrowed for the class for your state. Show them where to look for birthday and ID information, such as name, address etc. Show them the differences between over-21 and under-21 IDs.>

<Demonstrate with an ID as you explain.>

• Look to see that the laminate (plastic covering) is sealed all the way around. You will need to feel the ID for this, so have the guest take it out of a wallet. Curled corners or gaps in the seam may mean trouble; for example, someone pried it open and changed the details.

• Check to see that it is the original, not a duplicate license. In some states, a minor borrowing other identification from a legal-aged person can get a duplicate license while the legal person still uses the original. If it is a duplicate, ask questions.

• Look to see if the font (type of letters) is consistent within the license. Check that all of the lines line up.

• Check for the official seal or state name in off print within the ID. Check that all of the security tags are present.

If in doubt, ask some questions. Some good ones include:

<Have particiants practice these questions.>

What is your Social Security number?" (Only if on your state ID.)

"What organs are you donating?" (Usually on back, most states have a code, for eyes only, internal organs, etc.)

"What is your weight or height on this ID?" (Not something that people memorize.)

"What restrictions do you have for driving?" (All states with restrictive licenses, such as daytime only or glasses only, will have that on the license.)

Avoid asking address and birthday questions, as someone who has borrowed the ID will memorize those answers.

STILL DOUBTING THE VALIDITY OF THE ID?

Ask for secondary forms of ID. These secondary forms are carried in a wallet or purse and should match the information on the driver's license. Secondary ID will fall into two categories: photo or non-photo. Examples include the following:

Photo:

- College, school or university ID.

- Job-related picture ID.

- Social service cards, such as food stamps, etc.

Non-photo (except if it has a signature):

- Library card.

- Credit card.

- Some insurance cards, such as health insurance, car insurance, etc.

- Store cards for discounts on grocery if they have a signature.

Match the photo ID to the driver's license. Check to see if all of the information is the same and that the pictures and the person still look alike. For non-photo ID, check the signature on the card against the signature on the driver's license, and have the person sign in front of you. Check the third signature against both identifications.

 <Using your collection of secondary IDs, demonstrate how to compare those items with the ID. Show them how to check signatures.>

HOW DO MINORS BEHAVE? IDENTIFYING THEM EVEN IF THEIR IDS LOOK VALID

Sometimes a minor will acquire a fake ID, or will "borrow" an ID from someone who is of legal age. In this case, we are still serving a minor and are legally responsible. Part of your job is to look at the person as well as the ID. Identify minors by:

- Trendy outfits, sports teams, or "hip" dress.

- Ordering of "trendy" drinks — ones mentioned in TV programs or magazines.

- Remembering that underage drinkers like sugary drinks.

- No eye contact, looking away.

- Elaborate excuses or truly incredible tales to compensate for lack of identification.

Since their only experience with bars tends to be from watching TV and movies, minors will act like characters in one of those settings. Anyone who does not seem to know how to behave in a bar, so as to speak, may be a minor.

<Pose the following questions to your participants, and see if they come up with the correct answers.>

1. If a minor presents a fake ID and we let them drink without knowing they are a minor, are we still liable?

   Answer: Generally, yes; that is why you need to make completely sure that they are over 21.

2. I catch a minor with a drink. Now what should I do?

   Answer: Confiscate it.

3. Someone comes in claims that they left their ID at home. Now what?

   Answer: Refuse them entry and/or service.

 <This part walks them through how to handle common problems with minors. Modify based on your physical layout and house policies of your establishment.>

Scenario One

Someone comes up to the bar and orders a drink. They look young to the bartender. The bartender asks for ID, to which the customer replies, "They checked it at the door."

Suggested Responses

"I know, I have to check it anyway."

"I'm sorry, but house policy is that we need to check ID before serving drinks."

Goal: To aim for customer-friendly language, reiterating that the ID needs to be checked.

Scenario Two

Someone comes up to the bar and orders a drink. They look young to the bartender. The bartender asks for ID, to which the customer replies, "I left it in my car (at the house, at the table, etc.)."

Suggested Responses:

"I am sorry; I can't serve you until I see some ID."

"I am sorry; house policy won't let me serve you until I see some ID."

Goal: Again, to aim for customer-friendly language, but ID needs checking.

Scenario Three

A table of four is seated. The server checks ID, and two are 24 and the rest are 20. One of the legal-aged customers orders a pitcher of beer.

Suggested Responses:

"We are having a promotion on glasses of Miller Genuine Draft. Would you like a glass?"

Goal: To redirect customer focus onto a premium beverage without acknowledging the request for a pitcher.

"Sure, I can bring a pitcher with two glasses."

Goal: Acknowledges the request, yet makes it clear that only those of age should be consuming.

"I am sorry, house rules say I can't serve pitchers to tables with minors. How about a glass of draft?"

Goal: To acknowledge the request, but also inform the customer of house policies and give the customer a choice in order to keep the revenue.

Scenario Four

A server at a wedding sees a teenager drink a glass of beer. No adults are present at the table.

Suggested Response:

"Hi, I need to clear the drink glasses from the table. Could you give me that one in your hand?"

Goal: To make it clear that underage drinking is not allowed and the customers are being monitored.

"Hi, just checking to see if you need anything," said while clearing the table of drink glasses.

Goal: To use body language to inform the customer that the drinking will not be allowed and remove the glass to prevent it.

Scenario Five

Doorman is checking ID. An out-of state license <pick a state far away> is presented. Patron still looks young. Doorman says:

"So what are you doing in our town?"

Goal: To ascertain in a customer-friendly way why they are here and look for clues that they are underage.

"You know, we never had an ID from <state> before, do you mind showing me some other identification that you may have?"

Goal: To ask for additional identification in a friendly manner. If entrance is denied, the ID can be blamed for the denial.

Scenario Six

Bartender is checking ID and the customer looks young. Bartender asks:

"May I see some additional ID, please?"

Goal: To politely ask for more information.

Bartender has ID, plus a second ID, but still is not sure.

"Could you sign your name on this piece of paper – just checking."

Goal: To make it clear to the customer that a second verification is needed to ascertain age.

IDENTIFYING INTOXICATION

The second part of our laws means that we cannot serve intoxicated customers. In later modules we will talk about guests in our bar and strategies we use to make sure they do not get intoxicated. Now we need to focus on customers who show up at our bar and how we assess their intoxication level when they walk in the door. We do this so that we do not serve someone who is intoxicated, as we will be liable when they leave.

 <Have participants write the policies down as you explain them, or give them copies to look at while you explain them.>

Our house policies on guests who arrive intoxicated are:

<Explain house policies; emphasize that they need to leave without being served.>

Our cab companies are <cab company names and phone numbers. Also, include whatever pricing plan you have worked out with them. Explain that we need to call the cab company because we may be liable in case of an accident.>

Calling local authorities (police).

Call the local police if someone arrives in the red and then drives off after we deny service. If we are proactive in notifying officials, then there is a good chance they will catch those drivers before they cause harm.

IDENTIFYING INTOXICATION: ASSESSING GUESTS AT THE ENTRANCE

The goal of this part is to look at guests and assess their level of intoxication. Every guest who enters our establishment needs to be assessed before they are served. Each guest will be assigned a level: green, yellow, or red. Red guests cannot be served under any circumstances. Guest who arrive in the yellow <describe house policy here>; green guests are sober and can be served.

How to assess customers when they arrive and before you serve them:

1. Speak to them—ask questions and see how they respond.

2. Look at them—look them in the eyes and see if their pupils are dilated or glassy.

3. Look at their coordination – hand them a menu and see if they can open it. Look at how they are trying to light a cigarette or take a drink of water. If applicable, can

they take off their coats? Can they move around tables or are they bumping into things?

Yellow-Level Indicators:

- Overly friendly with other customers or employees.

- Speaks loudly or boisterously.

- Acts in an annoying manner.

- Belligerent or argumentative.

- Crude, uses lots of swear words.

- When you ask a question, does not answer or misunderstands the question.

- Very confrontational—hostile, aggressive toward staff.

- Makes irrational statements, and can't carry on a conversation.

Red-Level Indicators:

- They can't light a cigarette, or has two lit, or can't find the one they lit.

- Eyes are glassy and unfocused, pupils are dilated, will not look you in the eye.

- Speech is slurred, can't carry on a conversation. You

can see the effort it takes for them to figure out what they are going to say before they say it.

- Can't handle money.

- Can't stand up or walk. Stumbles, sways, staggers. Can't maneuver around items, such as doorways, chairs, or tables.

- Waves arms as if drowning.

- Falls asleep standing up or sitting down.

 <Walk the participants through the following scenarios.>

Scenario One

A customer shows up; he trips over the stairs on his way to the bar.

Response: He may just be clumsy; look for other indicators.

Scenario Two

The customer who tripped tries to light a cigarette while waiting to order. He just can't seem to get the match to his cigarette.

Response: He is probably in the red, deny service.

Scenario Three

Customer is spinning coins on a bar, yet is yelling loudly for the bartender.

Response: He may be obnoxious; coin spinning shows he is in control of his motor skills. Needs further assessment; may be in the yellow.

Scenario Four

Bartender says hi and asks for an order. Customer replies with a long-winded response about the last time they were here.

Response: He may just be a talker, or may have had a few drinks. Look for other indicators.

Scenario Five

Same customer won't look the bartender in the eye.

Response: He is probably in the yellow.

This part practices what happens if someone comes in and we assess them as being in the red. Some responses include:

 <Role-play — pick two or more participants to read the scripts until they are comfortable with the language.>

Scenario One

Customer comes in, obviously in the red.

Suggested Response:

"I am sorry sir; we cannot serve you this evening. I am calling a cab to get you home."

Goal: To be firm about service, yet recognize that he can't drive.

Scenario Two
Customer comes in, in the red, and turns to leave when they realize they won't be served.

Suggested Response:

"I am sorry sir; if you leave, I must call the police with your information."

Scenario Three
Customer arrives in the yellow.

Suggested Response:

"Hi, how would you like a nice plate of appetizers this evening?"

Goal: To delay getting a drink order to get food for the customer.

Scenario Four
Customer comes in, in the yellow, and orders a drink.

Suggested Response:

"Sure, just give me a minute to get it." Then be very slow in

getting it or divert to a task, such as ringing up the sale before serving it.

Goal: To delay getting the drink order to slow the customer's consumption.

 <Pose the following questions to your participants and see if they come up with the correct answers.>

1. Why should we call the police?

    Answer: If the person causes an accident, even though they did not drink here, we may still be liable. It is better to get them off the road than for this bar to be closed.

2. Our reputation is for fast, friendly service. Why be slow in serving customers in the yellow?

    Answer: We are simply re-prioritizing the order to assess the situation.

SUMMARY

We learned today:

1. Why we can't serve underage and intoxicated guests.

2. How to identify minors.

3. How to look at an ID and calculate legal age.

4. How to identify intoxicated customers.

5. Responses for dealing with certain situations, such as illegal IDs and customers we can't serve.

ASSESSING YOUR SKILLS

This is a quick test to see what you learned in this session. Answer each question by circling the correct answer.

1. A female customer comes in with an ID that has a ripped edge. She looks young. You need to:

   a. Ask for further identification.

   b. Ask her questions about what is on the ID she presented.

   c. Either, depending on the situation.

   d. Both.

2. A group of four guys comes into the bar. Three of the four have ID that looks valid, but the fourth one is suspect. You need to:

   a. Ask for further identification from the fourth person.

    b. Ask him questions about what is on the ID he presented.

    c. Both A and B.

    d. Deny the whole group entrance to the bar.

3. It is May 15, 2008. A customer shows you an ID with a birthday of February 2, 1988. Are they legal?

    a. Yes

    b. No

4. It is May 15, 2008. A customer shows you an ID with a birthday of September 13, 1987. Are they legal?

    a. Yes

    b. No

5. A customer has just handed you an ID. What three things do you look for?
    <List.>

6. A customer comes in slurring his words and can't light his cigarette. He may be:

    a. Green

    b. Yellow

c. Red

7. A man comes in and is fumbling at his wallet to find his ID. You need to:

    a. Immediately deny him service.

    b. Watch him for more clues to his status.

8. If we serve someone under the age of 21 in our state, then we risk:
   <Fill in the penalties.>

9. If we serve someone in our state who is intoxicated, then we risk:
   <Fill in the penalties.>

10. In our state, can third parties sue me (the employee) for damages?

    a. Yes, unconditionally.

    b. Yes, conditionally.

    c. Maybe, depending on the circumstances.

    d. No.

ANSWERS

In-Class Birthday Calculations

Legal:	Not Legal:
Chuck	Jimmy
Brian	Anne
Barb	Mike
Tony	
Pam	

Final Assessment

1. D – Depends on your house policies and types of fake ID that you usually get.

2. C – Only D if your operation does not allow minors in at all.

3. Yes, they are legal.

4. No, they are not legal.

5. Look at laminate, that it is in the original, correct font, and that the seal and state name are present.

6. Red.

7. B—watch him; he may just be clumsy.

8. Fill in penalties from earlier in the session.

9. Fill in penalties from earlier in the session.

10. Dram shop states will be A or B; common law states will be C or D.

MODULE 2

ALCOHOL AND THE BODY

INTRODUCTION FOR MANAGERS/OWNERS/ TRAINERS

This module covers how alcohol affects the body. It also explains why customers may behave as they do within the bar. Information that you need to collect before you teach this module includes:

- Copies of BAC charts from Chapter 1.

- Menus. Have your food menus ready to hand out. Make a list of items that are high in fat and protein, such as chicken strips and fried appetizers, that will help slow the effects of alcohol.

- List of outside companies that will deliver to your establishment for servers to hand out if you do not serve food.

- List of pre-packaged food. If you do not serve food but

can sell pre-packaged items, have them in-house and ready to go.

- A list of the alcoholic products that you serve, their proofs, and the average serving sizes for beers and wines.

- The DUI limit for your state from the Appendix.

- Your drink count charts from Chapter 1 and your drink recipes from Chapter 7. Make sure that your drink recipes reflect the BAC count.

ALCOHOL AND THE BODY – TRAINING MODULE

 ## MODULE OBJECTIVES—WHY DO I NEED TO KNOW THIS?

- It shows me how alcohol affects my customers.

- It shows me how tell if alcohol is affecting my customers.

- It shows me how to calculate drink equivalences for our bar.

- It shows me some of the factors that influence alcohol metabolism and how I can influence these factors to my advantage.

WHAT HAPPENS IN OUR BODIES WHEN WE TAKE A DRINK?

About 10 percent of the alcohol is absorbed in the mouth. The rest travels to the stomach where it waits in turn to go to the small intestine. Alcohol is absorbed, or moves through the small intestine walls directly into the bloodstream. The alcohol stays in the blood until the liver processes it. Since the liver can only process one drink per hour, all additional alcohol is stuck circulating in the blood until it is processed. When alcohol is in the bloodstream, it travels to the brain and begins interfering with the brain's activities. First, the part of the brain that controls logic, behavior, and inhibition is affected. After that, the alcohol will start affecting the part of the brain that controls bodily movement and control. Finally, if there is still alcohol circulating, it will begin to affect the part of the brain that controls breathing, heart rate, and other automatic functions. This alcohol keeps circulating until the liver is able to processes it and it is excreted out of the body.

<Using Figure 1, trace the path of alcohol through the body.>

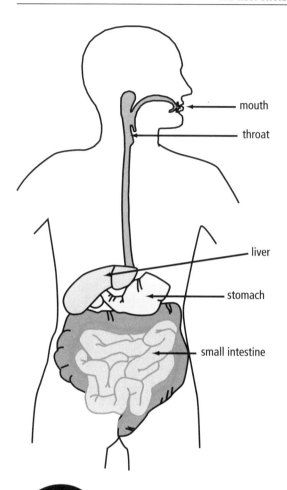

Why Is This Important?

If someone is drinking a lot, quickly, then all that extra alcohol affects more parts of the brain. You will begin to see the symptoms more quickly in a person.

WHAT TYPES OF ALCOHOL DO WE SERVE?

Most bars serve two types of alcohol. They are:

Fermented: Alcohol based on mashed plant material that is turned into alcohol. Beer and wine are the most popular fermented beverages.

Distilled: Some companies take alcohol from fermented mashes, heat it, and then collect the steam. The steam is heated and cooled several times, increasing the alcohol content each time it happens. Examples of distilled beverages include gin, vodka, whiskey, rum, liquors, cordials, and other alcoholic beverages.

 In our bar we serve: <Fill in with your most popular fermented and distilled beverages.>

 Proof measures how much alcohol is in a particular beverage. Proof is double the percentage of pure alcohol measured against water in a drink. For example, an 80 proof gin means that 40 percent of each serving is alcohol; the remaining 60 percent is water. An easy way to remember this is:

Proof ÷ 2 = percentage of alcohol

Why Is This Important?
Later in this module we will work on counting drinks, but be aware that a drink with a higher proof of alcohol will contain more alcohol than a lower-proof drink.

DRINK EQUIVALENCES

To make it easy to count drinks to estimate intoxication, the industry has an equivalency chart. These drinks are "equal" to each other, or they contain ½ ounce pure alcohol per serving.

- 12 ounces of beer

- One 4-oz glass of wine — usually 7–14 percent alcohol

- A drink made with 1¼ ounces of 80 proof liquor

- A drink made with 1 ounce of 100 proof liquor

 House Policies <Give them your recipes here for drinks, with the counts for each drink. Show sample of drink recipes. Stress using house recipes and pour devices.>

Pose the following questions to your participants and see if they come up with the correct answers.

1. Why do we need to use recipes and pour the same amount of alcohol in each drink?

   Answer: It will make it easier for you to count drinks, but it will also help in other ways. All drinks will be made the same way so that they will taste the same. This will help our customers, as they can expect the same-tasting drink each time. Customers like consistent drinks and will reward you with tips for them.

2. Why do we need to count drinks?

    Answer: Later in this module, we will work on how
    alcohol affects the body. Counting drinks will help you
    estimate your customer intoxication level. For example,
    how a person who drinks four drinks in one hour will
    act differently than someone who drinks four drinks in
    two hours.

3. But shouldn't a drink should count as one drink? Why
    do we need to calculate this new way of counting
    drinks?

    Answer: Because not all alcohol is created equal, and
    not all alcohol is served in the same way. Which do
    you think has more alcohol in it: a double Scotch on the
    rocks or a vodka and tonic? Answer: it depends. Which
    one is stronger depends on the proof of the Scotch,
    proof of the vodka, amount of Scotch poured and the
    amount of vodka poured. One drink could pack the
    same wallop as several other types of drinks, and you
    need to be able to figure out which are which.

4. What happens if the proof of liquor isn't 80 or 100
    proof? What is the count if we have a 16-ounce beer or
    a 6-ounce wine?

    Answer: The following charts will help.

BEER CHART		WINE CHART	
1 Drink = 12-oz Beer		1 Drink = 4-oz Wine	
Ounces	Number of Drinks	Ounces	Number of Drinks
6	0.500	3	0.75
8	0.660	4	1.00
10	0.875	5	1.25
12	1.000	6	1.50
14	1.160	7	1.75
16	1.330	8	2.00
18	1.500		
20	1.660		
24	2.000		

 For the beer and wine chart, simply highlight the glasses that you use to serve these items.

<Have participants fill in.>

In our bar, we serve <fill in> ounces of wine in a glass.

<Fill in> ounces of draft beer in a glass.

<Fill in> ounces of beer in bottles or cans.

LIQUOR CHART								
	Proof							
Ounces	30	50	60	80	90	100	120	150
0.50	0.150	0.250	0.300	0.400	0.450	0.500	0.600	0.750
0.75	0.225	0.375	0.450	0.600	0.675	0.750	1.000	1.220
1.00	0.300	0.500	0.600	0.800	0.900	1.000	1.200	1.500
1.25	0.375	0.660	0.750	1.000	1.130	1.250	1.500	1.875
1.50	0.450	0.750	0.900	1.200	1.350	1.500	1.800	2.250
1.75	0.500	0.875	1.000	1.400	1.500	1.750	2.000	2.500
2.00	0.600	1.000	1.200	1.600	1.800	2.000	2.400	3.000

In our bar, we serve: <Fill in> ounces of liquor in a straight drink (gin and tonic).

<Fill in> ounces of liquor in a shot drink (whiskey neat or on the rocks).

<Fill in> ounces of liquor in a juice drink (Screwdriver).

In our bar, our well liquors are:

<Fill in with type and proof.>

In our bar, our call liquors are:

> <Fill in with type and proof.>

In our bar, our top-shelf liquors are:

> <Fill in with type and proof.>

 <Go through the following scenarios and help participants calculate the drinks. Use the charts if needed. Make sure that they have the answers to John, Mary, Sara and Joe correct, as they will need them later in this session.>

Scenario 1: You are serving 1½ ounces of 100 proof gin with 3 ounces of tonic. How many drinks is this?

Scenario 2: You are serving a 20-ounce draft beer. How many drinks is this?

Scenario 3: You are serving a 6-ounce glass of wine. How many drinks is this?

Scenario 4: John, over the course of two hours, has consumed two 12-ounce beers, plus three 1-ounce shots of 80 proof whiskey. How many drinks has he had?

Scenario 5: Mary, over the course of three hours, has had three martinis made with 2 ounces of 150 proof gin. How many drinks has she had?

Scenario 6: Sara, since she arrived an hour ago, has had two glasses with 8 ounces of wine. How many drinks has she had?

Scenario 7: Joe has drank a Long Island Iced Tea, made with 1 ounce of 80 proof rum, 1½ ounces of 150 proof vodka and 1 ounce of 50 proof triple sec, along with 4 ounces of cola. How many drinks is this?

<Have participants write down or fill in.>

House Policies: In our bar, we keep track of how many drinks customers have had by <fill in, possible answers include POS, checks in front of customer, in pocket. >

HOW DRINK COUNTS RELATE TO BAC AND DUI

Blood alcohol content measures how much alcohol is in someone's body at a given point in time. BAC is a percentage, so 0.10 means that one drop of alcohol is present in 1,000 drops of blood. The only way to know someone's true BAC is by drawing blood or giving them a breathalyzer test.

BAC is the level used to determine whether a person is intoxicated. All states have laws that tell law enforcement what BAC level constitutes legal intoxication. If a person who is driving is pulled over and tested and is above the level, they can be arrested for "driving while under the influence" or DUI.

In our state, the DUI level is <fill in> BAC.

Understand that even if a person is not driving, if they are legally drunk and you served them their drinks, then you are still liable for damage they incur. For example, if you are a bartender in a hotel bar and serve someone beyond the point of intoxication, and they fall and injure another customer while walking back to their room, you are still liable.

The goal is to encourage our customers to have good time without leaving legally intoxicated.

So, how do you know if someone is intoxicated if you can't determine someone's BAC?

There are several ways to do this. First, we use what are called approximation charts. These charts show what behavior is associated with approximately what BAC level. A standard chart is:

<Make a copy of the chart and hand out. Explain or act out each level.>

BLOOD ALCOHOL CONTENT LEVEL	
.02	Warmth and relaxation of the customer.
.04	Individuals feel relaxed, soothed, and are talking more freely. Skin may show some flushing. May begin to remove outer clothing or complain that the temperature is "too hot."
.05	First signs of changes in behavior are observed. Lightheartedness, giddiness, lowered inhibitions. Restraint and judgment are impaired, coordination is altered, and moods may swing.
.06	Judgment may become impaired. Reaction time is slower. Maneuvering and making decisions is obviously impaired.
.08	Coordination is impaired and reaction time is slower. Driving ability is suspect. Cheeks and lips are numb. Hands, arms, and legs may tingle and then feel numb. This is the lower legally drunk level in some states.
.10	Clumsy; speech may become fuzzy. Reaction time and muscle control are deteriorated. Legally drunk in the rest of the states, and it is illegal to operate a motor vehicle with this or greater BAC in all states.
.15	Balance and movement are impaired.
.20	Motor and emotional control centers measurably affected; slurred speech, staggering, loss of balance, and double vision can occur.
.30	Lack of understanding of what is seen or heard; individual is often confused on his or her actions. Consciousness may be lost at this level; that is, individual "passes out."

BLOOD ALCOHOL CONTENT LEVEL	
.40	Usually unconscious; skin clammy.
.45	Respiration slows and can stop altogether.
.50	Can result in coma or death.

 Notice the shading on the chart? (Note: color chart is on companion CD-Rom.) They match the colors of a stoplight: green means go—or they can have a drink. Yellow means caution— need to go slow on the drinks. Red means stop—no more for the guest. This is the same as in the last session—Module 1 – assessing customers for intoxication before they arrive.

How Many Drinks Will Get Someone to This Level?

To follow are two charts: one for men, the other for women. You have to take a guess as to how much someone weighs, but this chart will show how the approximate number of drinks it takes to get to a certain BAC level.

 <Hand out copies of the two charts. Announce where the charts will be posted in the facility.>

BLOOD ALCOHOL CONTENT CHART—MEN	
1 Drink = 12-oz Beer	1 Drink = 4-oz Table Wine
1 Drink = 1-oz 100 Proof Liquor	1 Drink = 1-oz 80 Proof Liquor

These charts have a one-drink-per-hour elimination factor.

For Men	After 1 Hour of Drinking						
	Weight						
Drinks	120	140	160	180	200	220	240
1	.015	.010	.007	.004	.002	.001	.000
2	.046	.036	.030	.024	.020	.018	.014
3	.077	.062	.053	.044	.038	.035	.029
4	.108	.088	.076	.064	.056	.052	.044
5	.139	.114	.099	.094	.074	.069	.059
6	.170	.140	.122	.104	.092	.086	.074
7	.201	.166	.145	.124	.110	.108	.089

For Men	After 2 Hour of Drinking						
	Weight						
Drinks	120	140	160	180	200	220	240
1	.000	.000	.000	.000	.000	.000	.000
2	.030	.020	.014	.008	.004	.002	.000
3	.061	.046	.037	.028	.022	.019	.013
4	.092	.072	.060	.048	.040	.036	.028
5	.123	.098	.083	.068	.058	.053	.043
6	.154	.114	.106	.088	.076	.070	.058
7	.185	.150	.129	.108	.194	.087	.073

For Men	After 3 Hours of Drinking						
	Weight						
Drinks	120	140	160	180	200	220	240
1	.014	.004	.000	.000	.000	.000	.000
2	.045	.030	.021	.012	.006	.003	.000
3	.076	.056	.044	.032	.024	.020	.012
4	.107	.082	.067	.052	.042	.037	.027
5	.138	.108	.090	.072	.060	.054	.052
6	.169	.134	.113	.092	.078	.071	.057
7	.200	.160	.138	.112	.096	.088	.072

The chart for women is

BLOOD ALCOHOL CONTENT CHART—WOMEN	
1 Drink = 12-oz Beer	1 Drink = 4-oz Table Wine
1 Drink = 1-oz 100 Proof Liquor	1 Drink = 1-oz 80 Proof Liquor

These charts have a one-drink-per-hour elimination factor.

For Women	After 1 Hour of Drinking							
	Weight							
Drinks	100	120	140	160	180	200	220	240
1	.029	.021	.016	.012	.009	.006	.004	.002
2	.074	.058	.048	.040	.034	.028	.024	.020
3	.119	.095	.080	.068	.059	.050	.044	.038
4	.164	.132	.112	.096	.084	.072	.064	.056
5	.209	.169	.144	.124	.109	.094	.084	.074
6	.253	.206	.176	.152	.134	.116	.104	.092
7	.299	.243	.208	.180	.159	.138	.124	.110

For Women	After 2 Hours of Drinking							
	Weight							
Drinks	100	120	140	160	180	200	220	240
1	.013	.005	.000	.000	.000	.000	.000	.000
2	.058	.042	.032	.024	.018	.012	.008	.004
3	.103	.079	.064	.052	.043	.034	.028	.022
4	.148	.116	.096	.080	.068	.056	.048	.040
5	.193	.153	.128	.108	.093	.078	.068	.058
6	.238	.190	.160	.136	.118	.100	.088	.076
7	.283	.227	.192	.164	.143	.122	.108	.094

For Women	After 3 Hours of Drinking							
	Weight							
Drinks	100	120	140	160	180	200	220	240
2	.042	.026	.016	.008	.002	.000	.000	.000
3	.087	.063	.048	.036	.027	.018	.012	.006
4	.132	.100	.080	.064	.052	.040	.032	.024
5	.177	.137	.112	.092	.077	.062	.052	.042
6	.222	.174	.144	.120	.102	.084	.072	.060
7	.267	.211	.176	.148	.127	.106	.092	.078

 Remember the questions earlier on calculating drinks? Using the same customers, now with their weight added, what is their approximate BAC level?

<These are the same as the earlier examples, only weight is now included. Have participants calculate the BAC. May take several steps (drink by drink) to find the answers.>

Scenario 1: John, over the course of two hours, has consumed

two 12-ounce beers, plus three 1-ounce shots of 80 proof whiskey. John weighs about 220 pounds. What is his approximate BAC level?

Scenario 2: Mary, over the course of three hours, has had three martinis made with 2 ounces of 150 proof gin. She weighs about 180 pounds. What is her approximate BAC level?

Scenario 3: Sara, since she arrived an hour ago, has had two glasses with 8 ounces of wine. She weighs about 100 pounds. What is her approximate BAC level?

Scenario 4: Joe has drank a Long Island Ice Tea, made with 1 ounce of 80 proof rum, 1½ounces of 150 proof vodka and 1 ounce of 50 proof triple sec, along with 4 ounces of cola. He weighs about 200 pounds. What is his approximate BAC level?

Another question: Of the four customers above, who cannot legally drive now in our state?

FACTORS THAT INFLUENCE A PERSON'S BAC LEVEL

The charts are approximations; not everyone metabolizes alcohol in the same way. Look at the example above: Mary and Joe weigh about the same. Pretend that they just arrived at the bar. How many drinks in one hour will it take Joe to be legally intoxicated? How many drinks for Mary in that same hour? Men and women process alcohol differently; even at the same weight, Mary will feel the effect faster than Joe will.

Some factors that affect BAC levels are out of a server's control. They include:

Rate of Consumption

On average, a man will drink one drink every 30 to 55 minutes, with women taking a little longer, usually 40 to 45 minutes per drink. If someone drinks faster than this rate, they will show the signs of intoxication faster.

Take Steve for example. He is in your bar for two hours, weighs about 200 pounds and consumes six 12-ounce beers in that time. What is his BAC when he leaves? <Wait for answer.>

Now Tom arrives. He weighs the same amount and stays for two hours, but drinks ten 12-ounce beers in that time. What is his BAC level? <Wait for answer.>

Since the liver can only process one drink per hour, when Joe leaves one-third, or two out of his six drinks, have been processed, compared to Tom who has only processed 20 percent of his drinks, or two out of ten. Tom will be showing signs of intoxication much faster and more visibly than Joe will. It will take much longer for Tom's liver to metabolize all of the alcohol.

Part of your job as a server is to watch how fast the customer is drinking and slow them down if necessary. In later modules we will go over strategies which will help to slow them down.

Binge Drinking

Binge drinking is where a customer drinks very rapidly, in a short period, to increase the effects of alcohol. Binge drinking is popular with college students and others who want to get drunk faster.

Body Fat

Alcohol may pass easily through muscle tissue, yet not so easily through fat. Therefore, leaner, more athletically built customers may have a lower BAC than customers with more body fat even though the two weigh the same.

Body Size

The bigger, and generally the heavier, the customer, the more blood is in their body, thus drink for drink their BAC chart shows lower levels than a smaller person.

Age

The older people get, the more their enzymes and liver tend to slow down, and it may take longer than one hour to process a drink. Older patrons may also be on medication that affects how the alcohol is absorbed.

Sex

Female hormones make a difference in how alcohol is metabolized in the body. Women are also smaller and have more body fat than men of the same size, resulting in alcohol affecting them faster.

Medications

Most medications—both prescription and over the counter—will affect the absorption of alcohol, or alcohol will cancel out the benefits of the medication. If someone is on medication, they should not consume alcohol without their doctor's consent. Servers should keep an eye on any customer who looks ill (they may have taken some medicine) or who takes medication while at our bar. We may want to slow service to them.

Drugs

Illegal drugs and alcohol do not mix. If we suspect or see someone using an illegal drug, we need to stop service and call for a manager.

Level of Happiness

A customer who is calm and happy will probably have a lower BAC rate than a guest who is upset. If you see a guest who is upset, watch their consumption carefully.

FACTORS THAT A SERVER CAN INFLUENCE

Serve Food

Food in the stomach helps slow the absorption of alcohol. Offering food to our customers is one way to slow the rate.

<Have participants go through the menu. Guide them toward foods that are high in fat or protein. If you do not serve food, then give them a pre-packaged single serving snack or call in order information.>

Suggest items based on our menu include: <Fill in.>

Carbonated Drinks

Fizzy bubbles help to speed the alcohol through the stomach and into the small intestine. Watch customers who are drinking soda drinks (rum and Coke) or sparkling wines, as they might affect them faster.

Amount of Alcohol in the Drink

Consider how much the alcohol in the drink will affect a person's metabolism. This is why we went through the exercises earlier to calculate the number of drinks. Some of our drinks will count as one drink, others as two. Watch how many drinks you are serving per person. This is why we need to use standardized drink recipes so we can have an accurate count of how much is consumed.

<Pose the following questions to your participants and see if they come up with the correct answers.>

Question 1: If someone is drunk, we just need to give them coffee to sober up.

Answer: No. The amount of alcohol in the blood will stay the same. All coffee or caffeine will do is wake them up, so now we have a wide-awake drunk. If the person leaves, their BAC level is still high and we are still liable.

Question 2: Some of our customers do not match the chart. We have seen some drink more and not act intoxicated. Now what?

Answer: Every person metabolizes alcohol in different ways. Some of our customers are bigger, or more experienced drinkers, or may have food in their stomach. The BAC level in their blood, however, will still be high, so even though they are not behaving as if they are intoxicated, they may be legally intoxicated.

Question 3: What causes hangovers?

Answer: A variety of factors cause hangovers and their severity. The more alcohol a person drinks, the more dehydrated they get, and this lack of water in the body can contribute to their hangover. As the liver processes the alcohol, any sugars in the body have to wait to be processed. This excess sugar is also circulating around the bloodstream, possibly causing problems. Another possibility is some of the ingredients in the beverage—flavor agents, preservatives, colorings—may contribute to a person's headache.

Question 4: What if we have someone who we think has crossed the line over to alcoholism? How do we tell?

Answer: Alcoholism is a medical condition, and since we are not doctors, we should not try to diagnose people. If any of you have regulars who you are concerned about, bring their name and changes in their behavior to management's attention, who will sit down with the customer to discuss their behavior and possible action that may be taken.

Recap

In this session we learned:

- What happens to our bodies when we drink.

- What sample drink recipes look like and why we need to use them.

- How to calculate drink equivalences.

- How to count drinks and determine the approximate BAC levels of our customers.

- Which factors can affect how someone metabolizes alcohol.

ASSESSMENTS

This is a quick test to see what you learned in this session. Answer each question by circling the correct answer or filling in the blank.

1. When someone is drinking, the liver can only excrete one drink per hour. All other alcohol is doing what?

2. The heavier someone is, the more likely they will become drunk faster.

    a. Yes.

    b. Depends, are they heavy-set?

    c. No.

3. A man and a woman are drinking, matching drink for drink over the course of a couple of hours. Chances are:

    a. The woman's BAC is higher.

    b. Both of them have the same BAC.

    c. It depends upon their weights.

    d. The man's BAC is higher.

4. You have a new vodka which is 150 proof. How much alcohol by volume is this?

5. Tom orders a 20-ounce draft beer. How many drinks is this?

6. Peggy orders three glasses of 4-ounce wine in two hours. How many drinks has she had?

7. Jonas orders two 16-ounce draft beers, one rum (80 proof, 1 ounce) and Coke, and two "Slippery Nipple" shots made with 1½ ounces of 100 proof liquor. How many drinks has he had? If he drank these over the course of two hours and weighs 180 pounds, what is his approximate BAC?

8. Mary has been drinking steady for a while now and you want to suggest some food to her. From this menu, pick the best item:

a. Potato chips and pretzels.

b. Ham sandwich with French fries.

c. Veggie combo—battered-fried vegetables served with marinara sauce.

d. Veggie combo—various field greens melted with organic cheeses, served in a homemade tortilla roll.

9. Violet is a regular at your bar, coming in at least three times a week for a drink or two. Most nights, she is fine when she leaves; tonight it seems as if the same alcohol has really hit her. Some things you may want to look at or for include: <fill in>

10. Susie is drinking wine, Fred is drinking vodka and orange juice. How much of each is the equivalency of one drink? <fill in>

Answers:

First set of scenarios:

1. 1½ ounce 100 proof gin equals 1½ drinks

2. A 20-ounce draft beer equals 1.66 drinks.

3. A 6-ounce glass of wine equals 1½ drinks.

4. John has had two drinks (beer) plus 2.4 drinks (3 shots

x 0.8) for a total of 4.4 drinks.

5. Mary has had nine drinks. One martini made with 2
    ounces of 150 proof gin counts three drinks, multiplied
    by the three martinis is the equivalent of nine drinks.

6. Sara, four drinks. Each glass of wine is the equivalent
    of two drinks.

7. Joe's Long Island Ice tea is 1 ounce of 80 proof rum,
    (0.8 drink) plus 1½ ounces of 150 proof vodka (2.25
    drinks) plus 1 ounce of 50 proof triple sec (.5 drink) for
    a total of 3.55 drink equivalency.

Scenarios repeated with weight and BAC:

1. John, 4.4 drinks, two hours, weighs about 220 pounds.
    BAC level is approximately between 0.036 and 0.053.

2. Mary, nine drinks, three hours, weighs 180 pounds, her
    approximate BAC level would be more than 0.152

3. Sara, four drinks, one hour, weighs 100 pounds, her
    approximate BAC level would be 0.164.

4. Joe, 3.55 drinks, one hour, weighs 200 pounds, his
    approximate BAC level is between 0.044 and 0.064.

Cannot legally drive:
Mary and Sara cannot drive in any state.
John and Joe are below the 0.08 level, which is the lower BAC
level at this time.

Comparison—Sex and BAC Section:
Using 180 pounds as a comparison weight, Joe could drink five drinks in one hour and be legally intoxicated in .08 states and six drinks to be legally intoxicated in 0.10 states.

Mary would be legally intoxicated in 0.08 states after four drinks and legally intoxicated after five drinks in 0.10 states.

Comparison—Rate of Consumption:
Steve, two hours, weighs 200 pounds, six 12-ounce beers, his approximate BAC level is 0.076

Tom, 200 pounds, two hours, drinks ten 12-ounce beers, his approximate BAC is more than 0.094.

Assessment answers:

1. Excess alcohol that is not being processed is hanging out in the bloodstream circulating through the body and affecting the brain and its functions.

2. B: If they are heavier, they will have a lower BAC.

3. A or C: Generally, the woman will have a higher BAC, unless she is very big in comparison to her male companion.

4. Seventy-five percent alcohol by volume (proof divided by two).

5. 1.66 drink equivalency.

6. She has had three drinks.

7. First, calculate the number of drinks:

Two 16-ounce beers	= 2.66 drinks
One 1-ounce rum 80 proof	= 0.8 drink
Two 1½-ounce 100 proof	= 3 drinks
Total	**6.46 or 6.5 drinks**

   Next, use the male chart, 180 pounds; after two hours of drinking, his BAC would be between 0.118 and 0.143.

8. From this menu, the fried veggie combo (c) and ham sandwich (b) would be the best choices. If your establishment does not serve food, then many of the participants will want to answer (a), as it is applicable to your situation. Choice (d) — unless it was the only food at your establishment — is the worst of the four choices.

9. Viola may be affected by medication that she is on, or by her level of happiness. By having a conversation with Viola, you may be able to get a better sense of what is happening.

10. For Susie, one drink is equal to one 4-ounce glass of wine; for Fred, 1 ounce of 100 proof vodka or 1.25 ounces of 80 proof vodka would be one drink.

ALCOHOL AWARENESS POSTER: One Drink Equals

Posters are printed in full color and laminated to reduce wear and tear. It measures 11" x 17". Available from Atlantic Publishing, Item # ODE-PS, $9.95. To order, call 1-800-814-1132 or visit www.atlantic-pub.com.

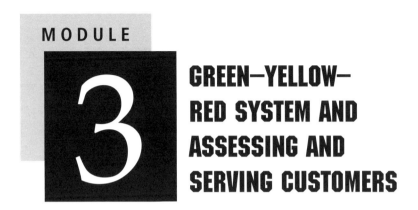

GREEN—YELLOW—RED SYSTEM AND ASSESSING AND SERVING CUSTOMERS

INTRODUCTION FOR MANAGERS/OWNERS/TRAINERS

This module explains your house policies. It covers strategies that may be used by employees to assess customers with the different levels of intoxication. As this is a long module, breaks are suggested before covering each color. Information that you need to collect before you teach this module includes the following:

- A list of suggested up-selling alternatives for all well liquors.

- A premium beer promotion setup.

- Signs and table tents for your signature cocktail.

- Drink recipes for all of your most popular drinks, with the applicable drink equivalence count and assigned glass.

- A list of nonalcoholic drinks available, printed on table tents.

- A food menu for the bar.

- If you can't serve food, then the preferred delivery place, or single-serve items, or cheap popcorn and peanuts to hand out.

- Posy-pourers installed and automatic dispensing equipment on order.

- Different-colored glasses for nonalcoholic drinks.

- Written policies on stacking, shots, pitchers, last call, water, free drinks, trays, waiting for order, and slowing service.

- Local cab company number programmed into phone and posted near pay phones. Signs/table tents are posted.

- Suggestions for service from Chapter 4.

GREEN–YELLOW–RED SYSTEM AND STRATEGIES FOR THEIR USE

MODULE OBJECTIVES—WHY DO I NEED TO KNOW THIS?

- How to assess customers.

- Which service methods work for different level of customers.

- What works best with customers who are in the green?

- What works best with customers who are in the yellow?

- What works best with customers who are in the red?

- What are our house policies on shots, pitchers, and last call?

- Overview of some of the programs that we sponsor.

WHAT IS THE GREEN–YELLOW–RED SYSTEM?

It is a way of assessing our customers and matching their approximate intoxication levels to our serving policies. Using the green–yellow–red system means that we can better serve our customers and keep our bar legally safe.

ASSESSING CUSTOMERS

This is a review of Module 2 – Assessing Customers. Here we will go into more detail.

Assess customers when they arrive and before they are served.

1. Speak to them—ask questions and see how they respond.

2. Look at them—look them in the eye and see if their pupils are dilated or glassy.

3. Look at their coordination—hand them a menu and see if they can open it. Look at them as they try to light a cigarette or take a drink of water. Can they take off their coats? Can they move around tables, or are they bumping into things?

Green Level—May Be Served

- Looks and acts sober.

- May act relaxed.

- No visible signs of intoxication.

- Goal: keep out of yellow.

Yellow Level—Serve with Caution, Begin Intervention

- Overly friendly with other customers or employees.

- Speaking loudly.

- Acting in an annoying manner.

- Belligerent or argumentative.

- Crude and using lots of swear words.

- When you ask a question, does not answer or misunderstands the question.

- Very confrontational — hostile, aggressive toward staff.

- Making irrational statements, can't carry on a conversation.

- Goal: keep out of the red.

Red Level—No Service Allowed, Begin Getting Them out Without Compromising Their Safety

- If they smoke, they can't light a cigarette, or have two lit, or can't find the one they lit.

- Their eyes are glassy and unfocused and pupils are dilated. They won't look you in the eye.

- Their speech is slurred and they can't carry on a conversation. You can see the effort it takes for them to figure out what they are going to say before they say it.

- They can't handle money.

- They can't stand up or walk. They are stumbling, swaying and staggering. They can't maneuver around items, such as doorways, chairs, or tables.

- They are waving their arms as if drowning.

- Goal: to get them home safely.

<Demonstrate or act out what green, yellow, and red guests behave like.>

GREEN GUESTS

Serving goal: To allow the customer to have fun without progressing to yellow.

SERVING SUGGESTIONS FOR GREEN GUESTS: OVERVIEW

- Up-sell.

- Serve water.

- Ask for food order or give free items.

- Offer signature drinks.

- Offer nonalcoholic drinks.

- Provide activities.

- Don't stack drinks.

- Wait for customer to ask for re-orders.

- Have drink recipes.

- Keep count of drinks served to each person; keep a tally with their approximate weight.

- Use different glassware for different types of drinks.

DETAILS OF SERVING METHODS

First Method: Up-Sell

Sell a customer on a premium beverage instead of regular well items. You get a higher tip.

< Have two people demonstrate the following scenario.>

Customer: "I want a gin and tonic."

Bartender: "We have Bombay, Beefeater and Tanqueray. Which do you prefer?"

Customer: "Oh, I'll have the Bombay, thanks."

How does this relate to you? <Fill in with prices from your establishment.>

2 well gin and tonics $2.50 ea. $5 total   20% Tip is $1
2 Bombay Gin and Tonics $3.00 ea. $6 total   20% Tip is $1.20

You've just made an extra 20 cents without trying.

<Give them the list of up-sell liquors based on your operation. Have them practice with one another (one as customer, one as server) and go through options on the list.>

How does up-selling work?

Since the customer is getting better alcohol, they will drink it more slowly than a well drink. The customer is appreciative that you asked what he preferred instead of serving the well. The customer is more likely to see you in a positive light: you are a friendly server. Customers do not want to get friendly servers "in trouble," so they will watch their consumption closely.

You have just increased your tip without any extra work.

Second Method: Serve Water

Serve a glass of water whenever anyone sits down, and keep it filled during the course of the evening. When customers drink water, it helps them to avoid dehydration. Drinking water will not cut down on alcohol consumption but will help customers deal with its side effects.

Third Method: Selling Food

Suggesting food does two things. Firstly, it increases your tab and tip, and secondly, food helps slow down alcohol absorption.

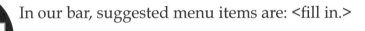

In our bar, suggested menu items are: <fill in.>

(If you have a food license, then give a list of appetizers. If you need to use pre-packaged items, show here with prices. If you are using free popcorn, peanuts, etc., mention now that they should be put out when people sit down.)

Fourth Method: Signature Drinks

Signature or special drinks are ones we are featuring:

<Show house signature drink, or this month's featured drink and the list for upcoming months.>

Why promote signature drinks? Customers want something special. They want something different from what they can get from the bar down the street. Signature drinks are what we are famous for, and people will pay for them.

Fifth Method: Nonalcoholic Drinks

We will promote nonalcoholic drinks on our menus and on table tents. Our goal is to have drinks available for those who do not want to drink alcohol.

Some sample nonalcoholic drinks that we have are <fill in.>

Sixth Method: Activities

To help slow consumption, we have activities in our bar. Activities encourage customers to have fun, and they will return to our establishment. Activities also help slow alcohol consumption by keeping customers busy.

Some activities include in our bar include <fill in.>

Seventh Method: No Stacking

Stacking is placing extra drinks in front of the customer, either because they order before they were finished, or because someone else sent them a drink. Allow only one drink per person at any one time. If someone has ordered a second drink, delay serving it until they are finished with their first.

<Have the participants practice wordings. Mix them up by having one participant act as the customer and another as the bartender.>

"I'll bring you the next one when this one is done. You don't want the beer to lose its head."

"I'll bring you the next one when this one is done. You don't want the soda to go flat."

"I'll bring you the next one when this one is done. I don't want the ice to melt."

If one customer buys a drink for another customer, use a <fill in> to hold the drink for them. Do not pour the drink until the receiving customer requests it.

Eighth Method: Wait for the Order

Waiting for the order means that we wait until the person asks for a drink, rather than asking early. If you feel that you need to ask the customer for a re-order, wait until they are finished with their drink. Waiting for the order does not mean you abandon the table, you simply do not ask for another drink order when stopping by and checking in until the glasses are empty. Some special circumstances that you need to watch include:

- Male–female pair: Wait until the woman is done before asking for the next drink. Asking after the man is finished means risking that the woman may have some drinks stacked up.

- Groups: Wait until at least two-thirds of the group is finished before asking for another drink. If you ask after the first one is finished, then you risk stacking the rest of the group.

Waiting means that faster drinkers will pause before they get their next drink. This will help slow their consumption, and you will avoid running back and forth to get the party members drinks.

Ninth Method: Drink Recipes

We have a drink recipe for each drink and a standard glass to match it. Examples of the recipes include:

 <Show a sample recipe, such as that for a margarita.>

 Reason for the recipes:

1. Standard taste for all customers.

2. Same amount of alcohol in each drink so we can count correctly.

3. Standard glass to match each drink

To go with the drink recipes, measure all alcohol with <fill in, jiggers or computerized system> devices to control the amount in each drink. Why? So, if need be, you can testify in a court of law how much was consumed. This protects you more than it protects the customer. If you have to testify that you did not use the standard pour devices, and that you free-poured, we risk the suit going against us. You may be fined based on your pouring.

All drinks will be served with standard recipes and in standard glasses. This is the only way we can be sure of what we have served to our customers.

Tenth Method: Keep Count

<Show servers how to track drinks. A sample log is on the next page. If you use POS, checks or some other system, show where they need to keep this information.>

SAMPLE LOG							
Server Log					**Day**	**Date**	
Table/ Seat	**M/F**	**Weight**	**# Drinks allowed**	**Drink Count and Time**			
				Count	**Time**	**Count**	**Time**
Bar #2	M	220 lbs	7d/2h	1.5	7 p.m.	1.5	8 p.m.

 In this table, 7d/2h is the bartender's abbreviation for seven drinks allowable in two hours based on weight. In the count columns, 1.5 is for 18-ounce draft beer (1½ drinks) and the time that they were served.

Other options instead of using the chart? Use the POS to keep track, or write times and drink equivalences on check.

 <Show participants a check and how you want it filled out. Show examples from cash register and POS system, if applicable.>

Eleventh Method: Different Glassware

Any nonalcoholic drink made, especially one that resembles a regular drink, is served in different glasses. This way we can identify drinks as alcoholic or nonalcoholic immediately. Minors should not be handling any glassware designated for alcoholic drinks.

<Demonstrate your alcoholic and nonalcoholic glasses so that everyone knows what they look like.>

Note: You probably will not use all methods for all customers, but rather a combination of them over the course of the evening. Except for drink recipes, glassware, counting and stacking, the method you use depends on your reading of the situation.

<Using your bar and your normal customers, discuss which techniques work best in different situations. Since there are so many variables in this area, a single general discussion will not work. In addition, introduce the specific suggestions in Chapter 4 to your employees.>

GOING FROM GREEN TO YELLOW

As customers continue drinking, they may progress from green to yellow. Some cues to watch for include the following:

- Becomes friendly with other customers or employees. Beginning to get "touchy."

- Speaks louder than in the beginning. Becomes more belligerent and argumentative when asked questions. Becomes hostile or aggressive toward employees.

- Acts in an annoying manner. Very demanding of service from the staff.

- Starts swearing and makes crude comments or suggestions. If a male, begins to hit on the female staff.

- When asked a question, not answering or misunderstanding the question.

- Makes irrational statements and being unable to carry on a conversation with the server.

- Shows definite signs of behavioral changes since initial assessment. Personality changes and becomes more erratic.

Signs like these suggest that the customer is moving into the yellow stage of intoxication and intervention needs to start.

SERVING YELLOW GUESTS

Yellow guests are feeling the effects of the alcohol and are on their way to becoming legally intoxicated. For these guests, you need to dramatically slow down the service and caution them that they will need to find an alternative to driving home. With this group, you must make sure that they do not move into the red.

SERVING SUGGESTIONS FOR YELLOW GUESTS: OVERVIEW

- Suggest food.

- Up-sell new drinks.

- No stacking.

- Slow service.

- Warnings.

DETAILS OF SERVING SUGGESTIONS

First Method: Suggest Food

Now is the time to push food. Make suggestions that it is time to eat, and ask for a food order. If they ask for another drink, counter with a food order.

 <Practice role-playing with various participants.>

Scenario:

Customer: "I'll have another beer."

Server: "Why don't you have one of our appetizers? The chicken wings with buffalo sauce are on special this week. They'll only take a minute or so for me to get."

Customer: "I'm not hungry, give me another beer."

Server: "I'm just concerned that you've been here for so long with nothing to eat. Besides, how can you visit us without trying our world-famous wings?"

 At this point, the customer will reply asking for another beer order, or begin to discuss food options with the server. If they persist with the beer order, then you need to make a decision concerning further service of the individual.

Second Method: Up-Selling

If a customer arrives in the yellow, then up-selling is a good technique to try. Emphasizing quality over quantity for a drink will help to slow the customer's drinking down.

 Customer (in the yellow): "I'll have a rum and Coke."

Bartender: "We have Captain Morgan's, Bacardi or Myers; what will you have?"

Customer: "I don't care, just give me a rum and Coke."

Bartender: Well, I'd love to make it, but which rum do you

want? Captain Morgan's, Bacardi or Myers? I want you to enjoy your drink."

Customer: "Ok, give me a Bacardi."

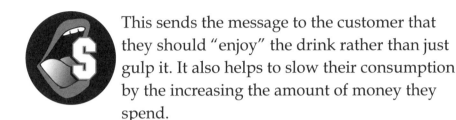

This sends the message to the customer that they should "enjoy" the drink rather than just gulp it. It also helps to slow their consumption by the increasing the amount of money they spend.

If a customer has been in your bar for a while, up-selling a well to call will not work at this point. What will work is an up-sell of another type of item.

Customer (few hours in your bar, in the yellow): "I'll have another beer."

Bartender: "Hey, Tom, we have this new drink that I think you'll like. We are trying it for our house specialty. It is a Citron Vodka with orange juice and a cherry twist. We are trying to get some customer feedback. Do you want to try it?"

Changing the beverage usually means that the drinker slows down consumption. Since the new drink is different from the old, they tend to savor it rather than gulp it. In addition, since you asked them their opinion, chances are they will give the drink due consideration and further slow down their drinking.

Third Method: Stacking

If someone is in the yellow, they should only possess one drink. Period. Do not allow stacking to occur if someone is in the yellow. If shots are going around, do not give one to a customer in the yellow in addition to a drink. They need to wait until their drink is finished. To prevent them from guzzling the drink for the shot, have all the shots wait until the customer is finished.

Fourth Method: Slow Service Strategies

Slowing service means that you become busy doing other necessary tasks and tell the customer "in a minute" or "hold on, I'm heading in your direction" to slow down the order.

 <Go through the following techniques and the suggested responses.>

Technique one: Talking to other tables and customers who are in the green.

Suggested response to the customer in the yellow: "Bill, let me get their order; I will be over in a minute."

Technique two: Bussing tables or sidework.

Suggested response: "I need to clear this table for another party; I will be over in a minute" or "Let me get more glasses (napkins, any item) because I can't serve you without them."

Technique three: Serving food or water — server's hands are full so they cannot take an order.

Suggested response: "John, I would love to get your drink order; I need to put these down and will be back."

Technique four: Bartender options — tapping the keg or fixing a line.

Suggested response: "Mary, I'd love to pour you another beer, but I need to fix the line. The beer's coming out all head."

Technique five: Need more alcohol.

Suggested response: "Sue, I'd love to get you another drink, but I need to run to the storeroom to get that vodka you wanted. Give me a minute, please."

 Aim for statements that make it seem as if you — as the bartender or server — are not abandoning your job, but rather that your job requires other tasks being completed, or you have other more pressing priorities. Indicating this to a customer, especially if it means "new" drinks for them, will help to keep them waiting.

Other slowing-service techniques can happen after the drink order is taken, but before the drink is served. Some suggestions include:

<Ask participants for other suggestions to slow service, in addition to those listed below.>

• Taking the long way to the bar and the long way back.

• At the service area, making the drink slowly, melding bottles before starting, cutting an extra lime garnish, and making it as slow as possible.

• Walking slowly to the bar, checking on other customers on your way to and back.

• Waiting in line for a drink to be made and putting all other drink orders ahead of this one.

The goal is to keep customers in view, but to make sure that their consumption is slowed by controlling how quickly their drink arrives. You want customers to perceive you as busy.

Fifth Method: Warnings

At some point, while a customer is in the yellow, you may wish to warn them that you are concerned about their consumption. Warnings may be needed if they made it into the yellow quickly and show no signs of slowing down. Make your warning to the customer alone, not in front of other guests or members of the party. Catch them on the way to the restroom or getting out of the chair.

 <Go through the following wordings with the participants. Watch for tone as they role-play with other participants. Have them practice until they get it right.>

"Sam, enjoy this one; I don't think that I can serve you another."

"Mary, you need to get something in your stomach. I am concerned about what you have had to drink so far, and you need something to absorb it. Let me get you an order of chicken strips."

"Sir, we generally don't serve this many drinks in this short of a period of time; perhaps you would care for a coffee or a soda?"

"Ma'am, I noticed you fell into the wall on the way to the ladies' room. Are you okay? Perhaps we need to try some water and popcorn for a while."

 Sometime the warnings need to go to other members of the party, especially if they are pushing drinks on someone. Some suggestions include:

 "Ma'am, I realize that this is the bride's last night out, but you have ordered five shots for her in the last hour. Do you want us to have to cut her off?"

Goal: To put the responsibility back on the person doing the ordering.

"Sir, I understand that you are hosting this party. We are concerned that several of your guests have had quite a bit to drink. We do not want to have to cut everyone off because of the way a few are acting. Perhaps it is time to order some food (or have dinner)."

Goal: To put the responsibility for the behavior of the guests onto their hosts.

"John, I know that you came in with Mary, and she is not looking good right now. Maybe it is time for some food or to go home."

Goal: To put the responsibility onto another member of the party.

<Pose the following questions to your participants and see if they come up with the correct answers.>

1. A man and woman have had an equal number of drinks. Now she is in the yellow, but he is still green. He is waving you over to get another round of drinks. Suggestions?

   Answer: Use the slow service, suggest food and use up-selling techniques.

2. They are saluting the bride-to-be with shots. She is definitely in the yellow, and the maid of honor has just

ordered another round for her. Suggestions?

Answer: Slow service, pull the maid of honor aside, and tell her that the bride needs to order her own drinks.

3. Two guys arrive in the yellow. They are yelling for beers. Suggestions?

Answer: Try up-selling them to another beverage.

 Sometimes, despite your best efforts, a customer will progress right into the red. Some cues to watch for that they have transitioned from yellow to red include the following:

- They are having problems smoking.

- They can't find their wallet or money; can't get money out of their wallet; can't figure out which bills they need to pay you with; or can't handle a credit card transaction.

- They can't carry on a conversation. They are very unfocused, with scattered thought processes. You are now hearing their stories for the second time this evening. Their words are slurred and they are using their arms to make points.

- Their eyes are glassy and unfocused, and their pupils are dilated. They won't look you in the eye.

- They can't stand up or walk. They are stumbling, swaying, and staggering. They can't maneuver around items, such as doorways, chairs or tables.

- They are falling "asleep" standing up or sitting down.

Do not serve guests who are in the red. No more drinks!

GUESTS IN THE RED

Arrives in the Red

You need to deny entrance to the bar in this situation. Once the customer is in, even if they do not have a drink, you may be liable. If they drove to your bar, you need to prevent them from leaving in their car. Some suggested wordings include:

<Practice with the participants until they are comfortable with this.>

"I'm sorry, sir; we won't be serving you this evening. I am calling a cab for you."

"I'm sorry, we cannot serve the lady. Perhaps it is time to drive her home," said to a sober companion.

"I'm sorry, but we are full and you won't be able to come in. We are calling a cab to take you home."

If the person refuses to take a cab, try the following:

"I'm sorry; we will need to notify the local authority if you leave. Perhaps you would like to wait for the cab?"

If the person leaves, call the police. Give them the name of the bar, location, car color, make and model. Have them give you the time and name of person who took the information from you.

Gets to the Red in Your Bar

Once someone is in the red, they need to be cut off. Suggested wording includes:

"I am sorry, we can't serve you anymore. Shall I call a cab for you?

If the customer protests, keep repeating the same phrase over and over again. Do not allow them to draw you into argument about why they are shut off. Sample dialogue includes the following:

<Have them practice this until they are comfortable with the wording.>

Server: "I am sorry, we can't serve you anymore. Shall I call a cab for you?"

Customer: "Why not? Give me another beer!"

Server: "I am sorry, we can't serve you anymore. Shall I call a cab for you?"

Customer: "You are serving him; give me one. Why can't I

have one?"

Server: "I am sorry, we can't serve you anymore. Shall I call a cab for you?"

Customer: "You are picking on me. There is no reason why I can't have one. Give me another beer."

Server: "I am sorry, we can't serve you anymore. Shall I call a cab for you?"

Keep repeating the same phrase over and over again.

 If possible, a second employee should be nearby to witness the situation and monitor for potential problems. Ideally, this should be a manager. If a manager is not available, a supervisor or another employee will do.

If a customer in the red begins to leave, then use the scripts from earlier to prevent them from driving. Call the police if necessary, as you need documentation that you attempted to prevent them from driving home.

If a customer is in the red and has passed out, call for medical treatment if their breathing is erratic or they are not responsive when you try to wake them up. If you can get them up, do not allow someone to give them another drink; instead focus on getting them home safely. Remember that the average person can only process one drink per hour, so a person who has passed out will be affected for several more hours. Err on the side of caution by calling for treatment if they are not responsive.

FORMS TO FILL OUT

<Show the participants your logs and what information that you want in them. Pass around a "dummy" book and have them record an incident. Make sure that they know which incidents to document.>

Why do we want you to fill this out?

•   Because as time goes on, people tend to forget details <ask them if they remember something from ten years ago, such as the Challenger accident or another major event in their life.>

• Because "contemporary" (when it happened) records tend to be favored in courts, rather than a report written later.

• Because this is for your protection as well as ours.

OTHER HOUSE POLICIES

Shots

<Give participants the house policy on shots, including how they are served, who is serving them, and times that they are available. If it is a special occasion, such as a birthday, then the guest of honor must order their own shots. No extra shots will be given. No shots during the

last hour of the evening.>

Pitchers

<Give participants the house policy on pitchers, including times that they are available and the minimum number of people at the table before they can be ordered. Clarify your policy on pitchers and minors at the table.>

Free Drinks

<Give participants the house policy on free drinks. If you give free drinks for special occasions, such as anniversaries, then address what can be given and by whose authority. If a customer is seeking something because of bad service, bad product, or a complaint, explain the free dessert or gift certificate for the next visit. Sample free drinks will be served by a manager in 1-ounce portions at specific times.>

Re-Entrance Policy

<If you have a cover charge, discuss how often a customer can leave and re-enter the premises. Discuss how you will track individual customers and their re-entrance. Discuss options if a customer wants to come back in after leaving too many times.>

Last-Call Policy

<Fill in with your last-call policies. Include times of announcements, instructions for bands, DJs, and lighting. Discuss drinks that will not be served, such as shots or pitchers. Explain how quickly customers need to be cleared out of the premises. Address calling cabs beforehand for customer use. Stress to valets the need to assess customers before they leave.>

PROGRAMS THAT WE HAVE DEVELOPED

We have developed the following programs for our customers that will help us create a legally safe atmosphere.

PROGRAM OVERVIEW

- Designated driver.

- Cab program.

- Nonalcoholic drink program.

Designated Driver

<Explain your bar's policy on designated drivers. Emphasize the price of sodas for the DD, what happens if the DD starts

drinking, how to identify the DD (pins, hand stamps.) Make it clear that just because there is a DD in the party, the others do not get to drink themselves into the red: we are still responsible for them.>

Cab Program

<Explain your cab program. Discuss calling the cab, who pays for it, and whether some cabs will be at the bar at closing time. If you have multiple cab companies in your area, discuss their participation.>

Nonalcoholic Drink Program

<Explain your nonalcoholic drink program. Hand out copies

of promotional materials. Explain how some people want to enjoy themselves at the bar but not necessarily drink. Explain how the pricing structure will work to their advantage for these drinks.>

RECAP

We learned:

- How to serve customers who are in the green.

- How to serve customers who are in the yellow.

- What to do with customers who are in the red.

- What to say in these situations.

- Our house policies on last call, designated drivers and other issues.

ASSESSMENT

Answer each question by describing how you would handle the situation. Describe the methods you would use to serve alcohol responsibly.

1. Two men have been in your bar drinking for about two hours. Both are now in the yellow. Six other people have just joined them and they ordered shots for everyone. They are celebrating promotions.

2. A customer sitting at your bar for several hours has progressed into the red without anyone noticing. He is now getting up to leave.

3. A group of four has just wandered over from the bar next door. One is the designated driver and is in the green, two are in the yellow and one is definitely in the red. The three who are drinking now want to order beers and shots.

4. You are a server in a popular beachfront bar. You are serving about forty customers spread across six tables. A party of eight has been drinking steadily all afternoon and has had several rounds of appetizers. Three of the party are in the yellow, starting to go to red, while the remainder are just in the yellow. They want to order another round of drinks.

5. Two friends sitting at the bar together have been quietly watching the baseball game. Since the home team lost, their mood is getting fouler by the minute. They now want to order more drinks.

6. A regular, who is a friend of the owner, likes to use his status as a regular to browbeat servers into keep serving him. He is now going into the red and demanding more drinks.

7. At a wedding reception, you notice a member of the bridal party slip a drink to an underage cousin.

8. A party of four arrives, all in the green. Three order beers, but the fourth seems hesitant to order a drink.

9. A romantic couple has been eating and drinking all night long. She is definitely in the yellow, while he is still in the green. He wants to order a split of champagne to celebrate.

ANSWERS

1. With the guests of honor in the yellow and new participants showing up, this is a tricky situation. Options include taking a food order, pulling aside one of the new arrivals and explaining the situation, or slowing service. Discussing the situation with a member of the party may be your best bet.

2. Use the lines from leaving section: calling a cab or calling the police. Review your shift changeover policies to make sure that oncoming staff knows everyone's status.

3. You may want to refuse the whole party entrance. Your goal is to make sure that the red guest does not get in or served in your bar. You may suggest that the designated driver takes him home.

4. Some suggestions include slowing service, serving more water, and perhaps free popcorn. Since they have eaten, suggesting food may not work in this situation. Your goal is to slow down service so that the guests near the red can metabolize what they have consumed.

5. If they are not in the yellow or red, then refusing service is not an option. You have the right to remind them to calm down.

6. Still refuse service. If the owner orders you to serve the drink, document it so that if something happens, your liability is mitigated.

7. Confiscate the drink. Speak to the person who slipped him the drink, and then if needed, inform the host of the event.

8. May not be a drinker or is tonight's designated driver. Explain the designated driver program at your bar or give him or her the nonalcoholic drink menu. If you suspect the hesitant party is a minor, check identification.

9. Delay service—offer to ice the champagne or take the long way around to get it. Your goal is to delay serving the drink.

ALCOHOL AWARENESS POSTER: We Check IDs

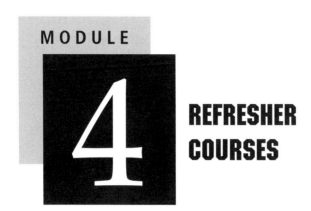

MODULE

4

**REFRESHER
COURSES**

INTRODUCTION FOR MANAGERS/OWNERS/ TRAINERS

After the initial three training sessions are completed, refresher courses are needed. Rather than being full-fledged session, refresher courses just touch on the main points of each section. This course is designed for servers who have been through the original three sections. It should last about an hour. Refresher courses may be offered once a quarter, depending on your personnel.

Read your incident logs on a regular basis, and if a theme seems to be emerging, such as not recognizing intoxication levels, problems with identifying minors, or not able to count drinks, you may wish to run the full module associated with that topic again.

REFRESHER COURSE

Review of legal issues.

<Note to managers: Dram shop states continue here, common law states skip to the similar section below.>

DRAM SHOP LAWS

We are in a dram shop state, which means our state laws on serving alcohol specify the following:

- It is illegal to serve someone who is a minor (under 21).

- It is illegal to serve someone who is intoxicated.

If we serve anyone in those two groups, we face:
<Circle>

Fines
Jail Time
Being Sued
All of the Above

Fines can range from $ <fill in> to <fill in.>

Jail time can range from <fill in> to <fill in.>

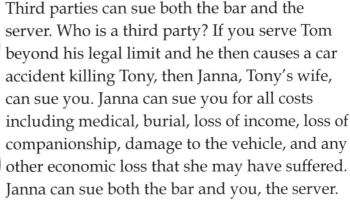

Third parties can sue both the bar and the server. Who is a third party? If you serve Tom beyond his legal limit and he then causes a car accident killing Tony, then Janna, Tony's wife, can sue you. Janna can sue you for all costs including medical, burial, loss of income, loss of companionship, damage to the vehicle, and any other economic loss that she may have suffered. Janna can sue both the bar and you, the server.

Note to dram shop state managers: Skip next section and go to Other Laws in Our State.

COMMON LAW STATES

We are in a common law state, which means that in our state:

- It is illegal to serve a minor (under 21)

- If we serve someone who is intoxicated, then we risk being sued if they cause an injury. If a reasonable person could see that the person was so intoxicated that they should not have driven, then we may be held liable (legally responsible).

In our state, third parties may be able to sue the bar and the server. Who is a third party? If you serve Tom so many drinks that he is obviously intoxicated when he leaves, and then Tom causes an accident which kills Tony, then Janna, Tony's wife, may be able to sue. She can sue for any economic costs associated with Tony's death if the lawsuit is successful.

IDENTIFYING MINORS

In our state, only the following IDs are acceptable: <list.>

In Class To-Do

<Have the class do the following examples on their own; check answers.>

Today is March 17, 2007. Are the following customers legal?

Chuck	12/7/42
Jimmy	1/4/87
Brian	2/10/86
Barb	5/8/70
Anne	9/3/90
Mike	10/6/86
Tony	1/23/85
Pam	10/14/83

<Review how to check IDs and identifying minors.>

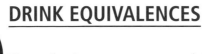

DRINK EQUIVALENCES

To make it easy to count drinks, the industry has an equivalency chart. These drinks are "equal" to each other or they contain a half ounce of pure alcohol per serving.

ONE DRINK IS EQUIVALENT TO:
12 ounces of beer
or
1 4-oz glass of wine—usually 7–14% alcohol
or
A drink made with 1 $\frac{1}{4}$ ounces of 80 proof liquor
or
A drink made with 1 ounce of 100 proof liquor

<Go through the following scenarios and help participants to calculate the drinks. Use the charts if needed. Make sure that they have the answers to John, Mary, Sara and Joe correct, as they will need them later in this session.>

Scenario 1: You are serving 1½ ounces of 100 proof gin with 3 ounces of tonic. How many drinks is this?

Scenario 2: You are serving a 20-ounce draft beer. How many

drinks is it?

Scenario 3: You are serving a 6-ounce glass of wine. How many drinks is it?

Scenario 4: John, over the course of two hours, has consumed two 12-ounce beers, plus three 1-ounce shots of 80 proof whiskey. How many drinks has he had?

Scenario 5: Mary, over the course of three hours, has had three martinis made with 2 ounces of 150 proof gin. How many drinks has she had?

Scenario 6: Sara, since she arrived an hour ago, has had two glasses with 8 ounces of wine. How many drinks has she had?

Scenario 7: Joe has drank a Long Island Ice Tea, made with 1 ounce of 80 proof rum, 1½ ounces of 150 proof vodka and 1 ounce of 50 proof triple sec, along with 4 ounces of cola. How many drinks is this?

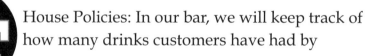 House Policies: In our bar, we will keep track of how many drinks customers have had by

<Fill in; possible answers include point-of-sale, checks in front of customer, in pocket.>

 In our state, the DUI level is <fill in> BAC.

ASSESSING CUSTOMERS

Assess customers when they arrive, before you serve them.

1. Speak to them — ask questions and see how they respond.

2. Look at them — look them in the eyes and see if their pupils are dilated or glassy.

3. Look at their coordination — hand them a menu and see if they can open it. Look at how they are trying to light a cigarette or take a drink of water. If applicable, can they take off their coats or outerwear? Can they move around tables or are they bumping into things?

Green Level—May Be Served

- Looks and acts sober.

- May act relaxed.

- No visible signs of intoxication.

- May be served; goal: keep out of yellow.

Yellow Level—Serve with Caution, Begin Intervention

- Overly friendly with other customers or employees.

- Speaking loudly, boisterous.

- Acts in an annoying manner.

- Belligerent, argumentative.

- Crude, using lots of swear words.

- When you ask a question, does not answer or misunderstands the question.

- Very confrontational—hostile, aggressive toward staff.

- Makes irrational statements and can't carry on a conversation.

Red Level—No Service Allowed, Begin Getting Them out Without Compromising Their Safety

- If they smoke, they can't light a cigarette, have two lit, or can't find the one they lit.

- Their eyes are glassy and unfocused and pupils are dilated. They won't look you in the eye.

- Their speech is slurred and they can't carry on a conversation. You can see the effort it takes for them to figure out what they are going to say before they say it.

- They can't handle money.

- They can't stand up or walk. They are stumbling, swaying, and staggering. They can't maneuver around items, such as doorways, chairs, or tables.

- They are waving their arms as if drowning.

- They are falling "asleep" standing up or sitting down.

SERVING SUGGESTIONS FOR GREEN GUESTS: OVERVIEW

- Up-sell.

- Serve water.

- Ask for food order or give free items.

- Offer signature drinks.

- Offer nonalcoholic drinks.

- Provide activities.

- Don't stack drinks.

- Wait for customer to ask for re-orders.

- Have drink recipes.

- Keep count of drinks served to each person; keep a tally with their approximate weight.

- Use different glassware for different types of drinks.

SERVING SUGGESTIONS FOR YELLOW GUESTS: OVERVIEW

- Suggest food.

- Up-sell new drinks.

- Don't stack drinks.

- Slow service.

- Offer warnings.

GUESTS IN THE RED

If they arrive that way, then they need to leave.

If they get that way in our bar, we need to make sure that they get home safely.

APPENDIX

A

ALABAMA	
Dram Shop State?	Yes
BAC Level	0.08
Age—Pour	21
Age—Sell	21 (19–20 restaurant license only)
Age—Serve	21 (restaurants with Responsible Vendor Certification can serve at 19–20)
Happy Hour Laws	No two-for-one promotions; same price, all day long.
Number of Drinks	Not regulated.
Max Alcohol per Drink	No established limit, but amount of alcohol in each drink must be posted.
Mandatory Server Training	Yes
Mandatory topics?	Yes

ALABAMA, con't

Notes on Training: The Responsible Vendor Program is voluntary for licensees. It costs $35 per license, per year. Licensees can complete an approved independent program and become registered with the state as a Responsible Vendor. Participation is voluntary, but suggested. The cost and length of time required for training varies.

Web/Contact for State	Alabama Alcoholic Beverage Control Board 334-271-3840 www.abcboard.state.al.us
Hours	On-Premise Drinking: 24 hours, except after 2 a.m. on Sunday; local regulations apply.

ALASKA	
Dram Shop State?	Yes
BAC Level	0.08
Age—Pour	21
Age—Sell	21 (19–20 restaurant license only)
Age—Serve	21 (restaurants with Responsible Vendor Certification can serve at 19–20)
Happy Hour Laws	No single-priced, unlimited service drink specials, free drinks for patrons or two-for-one drink specials. Cannot encourage or promote any organized game that awards alcohol as a prize or promotes excessive drinking. May offer a food and drink combination for a special price ONLY if the special is equal to or greater than the normal price of the drink.
Number of Drinks	2
Max Alcohol per Drink	Not regulated.
Mandatory Server Training	Yes
Mandatory topics?	Yes
Notes on Training: Requires all employees who serve or sell alcohol to complete an approved server-training program within 30 days of hiring and to be able to produce a certification card. The state approves programs.	
Web/Contact for State	Alaska Alcoholic Beverage Control Board 907-269-0350
Hours	On-Premise Drinking Monday–Saturday: 8 a.m. to 5 a.m., Sunday: 8 a.m. to 5 a.m.

ARIZONA	
Dram Shop State?	Yes
BAC Level	0.08
Age—Pour	19
Age—Sell	19
Age—Serve	19
Happy Hour Laws	No free drinks to patrons. Licensees may give away free drinks; may offer a food and drink combo for a special price. No difference between "happy hour," "drink specials," and/or "promotions."
Number of Drinks	See maximum alcohol per drink for serving amounts. Cannot serve more drinks than legal volume.
Max Alcohol per Drink	32-oz. beer; 1-liter wine; 4-oz. distilled spirits
Mandatory Server Training	No, but does have guidelines.

Notes on Training: Does not require server training, nor does the state provide a training program for licensees. However, the state does certify trainers of private programs to train Arizona Liquor Law. If a state-certified trainer in an approved program trains a licensee, fines and penalties for violations can sometimes be mitigated. Trainers in Arizona are required to use the Arizona Supplement as part of the training program and all servers must receive a certification of completed alcohol training programs form. Trainers can obtain this form from the Arizona Department of Liquor Licenses and Control. A basic and management-approved training class is now required for the person responsible for the day-to-day operations of the business. This requirement is only for new managers or for a new licensee application.

ARIZONA , con't	
Web/Contact for State	Arizona Department of Liquor Licenses & Control, 602-542-5141, www.azll.com
Hours	On-Premise Drinking: Monday–Saturday: 6 a.m. to 1 a.m., Sunday: 10 a.m. to 1 a.m.

ARKANSAS	
Dram Shop State?	Yes
BAC Level	0.08
Age—Pour	21
Age—Sell	21
Age—Serve	21
Happy Hour Laws	Licensees may not give patrons free drinks.
Number of Drinks	Not regulated.
Max Alcohol per Drink	Not regulated.
Mandatory Server Training	Yes
Notes on Training: Responsible Permittee Regulation: The maximum a trainer can charge for training is $25. Length of the program is up to the program provider.	
Web/Contact for State	Arkansas Alcoholic Beverage Control Board 501-682-8174, ABCAdmin@dfa.state.ar.us
Hours	On-Premise Drinking: Private Clubs: Class A: 7 a.m. to 2 a.m.; Class B: 10 a.m. to 5 a.m.; Restaurants: 7 a.m. to 1 a.m.; Sunday: Prohibited (local option possible)

CALIFORNIA	
Dram Shop State?	Yes
BAC Level	0.08
Age—Pour	21
Age—Sell	21
Age—Serve	21 for bartenders and cocktail servers, 18 to serve alcohol in a bona fide eating place, if working in an area primarily designed and used for the sale and service of food and as an incidental part of a server's overall duties.
Happy Hour Laws	No free drinks, two-for-one drink specials, or anything of value in conjunction with the sale of an alcoholic beverage. Permitted to offer a food and drink combo for a special price as long as the drink is not free or complimentary. The price paid for a meal alone must be less the price for a meal and an alcoholic beverage together. No difference between "happy hour," "drink specials," and/or "promotions" as these are generic terms used to describe reduced rates for drinks and are permitted as long as the retailer charges a price for the drink that does not undercut the wholesale price paid.
Number of Drinks	Not regulated.
Max Alcohol per Drink	Not regulated.
Mandatory Server Training	No

CALIFORNIA, con't

Notes on Training: No state laws regulating server training. Some cities or counties may require server training as part of their Conditional Use Permit process (for example, City of Dana Point in Orange County). The Department of Alcoholic Beverage Control offers a voluntary training program for licensees called LEAD (Licensee Education on Alcohol and Drugs). This program focuses its training efforts on new license applicants, licensees located in high-crime areas, licensees who have violated ABC laws, major special events and county fairs. This program is, however, open to all persons.

Web/Contact for State	California Department of Alcoholic Beverage Control, cust.serv@abc.ca.gov
Hours	On-Premise Drinking: Monday–Sunday: 6 a.m. to 2 a.m.

COLORADO	
Dram Shop State?	Yes
BAC Level	0.08
Age—Pour	18
Age—Sell	18
Age—Serve	18 [Note: to pour/serve must be supervised by someone who is 21—only in places where full meals are regularly served. Tavern employees must be 21 unless the tavern regularly serves meals.]
Happy Hour Laws	Not regulated.
Number of Drinks	Not regulated.
Max Alcohol per Drink	Not regulated.
Mandatory Server Training	Yes
Notes on Training: Colorado's Responsible Vendor Program went into effect on April 1, 2005. This program offers mitigating benefits to any licensee found to have served a minor during an established sting operation by the state and/or local licensing authority.	
Web/Contact for State	Colorado Dept of Revenue Liquor Enforcement Division, 303-205-2306, www.revenue.state.co.us/liquor_dir/home.asp
Hours	On-Premise Drinking: Monday–Sunday: 7 a.m. to 2 a.m.; no restrictions for on-premise sales on Sundays.

CONNECTICUT	
Dram Shop State?	Yes
BAC Level	0.08
Age—Pour	18
Age—Sell	18
Age—Serve	18
Happy Hour Laws	No single-priced, unlimited service drink specials or encourage/promote any organized game that awards alcohol as a prize or promotes excessive drinking.
Number of Drinks	One
Max Alcohol per Drink	Not regulated.
Mandatory Server Training	No
Web/Contact for State	Dept. of Consumer Protection, 860-713-6210, www.ct.gov/dcp/cwp
Hours	On-Premise Drinking: Monday–Thursday: 9 a.m. to 1 a.m.; Friday–Saturday: 9 a.m. to 2 a.m.; Sundays: 11 a.m. to 1 a.m. on-premises, unless changed by local ordinance.

DELAWARE	
Dram Shop State?	No
BAC Level	0.08
Age—Pour	21
Age—Sell	21
Age—Serve	19
Happy Hour Laws	No two-for-one drinks, drinks sold below cost, or given away free. May offer a food and drink combo for a special price. No difference between "happy hour," "drink specials" and/or "promotions."
Number of Drinks	No more than one alcoholic beverage may be sold to a person less than 15 minutes prior to closing each day that a license is open.
Max Alcohol per Drink	Not regulated.
Mandatory Server Training	Yes
Notes on Training: All who sell or serve alcohol, supervisors, and licensees if directly involved in the management of the premises to complete a mandatory server-training course. Servers must complete a course within 30 days of employment. An ID card is issued upon completion of the course and must be presented on request by an OABCC agent or employer; otherwise, the employee will be cited for a violation. The legislature passed a server training law for package stores slated to begin on January 1, 1998.	
Web/Contact for State	Delaware Div. of Alcoholic Beverage Control, 302-577-5222, www.state.de.us/dabc

DELAWARE, con't
Hours	On-Premise Drinking: Everyday: 9 a.m. to 1 a.m.; Sundays: 9 a.m. to 1 a.m. for restaurants.

DISTRICT OF COLUMBIA	
Dram Shop State?	No
BAC Level	0.08
Age—Pour	21
Age—Sell	18
Age—Serve	18
Happy Hour Laws	Licensees may not offer two-for-one specials.
Number of Drinks	One per regulations, backup drinks include second drinks served as part of a "two-for-one" promotion, second drinks served just prior to last call and second drinks provided complimentary by the licensee or purchased by other patrons. Except as provided above, backup drinks do not include two different drinks served together, such as a beer and a shot or any other industry drink that can be considered a shot and a mixer. The prohibition against backup drinks also does not apply to the service of wine with a meal where the patron has not finished a previously served cocktail.
Max Alcohol per Drink	Not regulated.
Mandatory Server Training	Yes
Notes on Training: Effective September 30, 2004, the District of Columbia has a mandatory training program for managers of on-premise establishments.	

DISTRICT OF COLUMBIA, con't	
Web/Contact for State	Dept. of Consumer & Regulatory Affairs, Alcohol Beverage Div., 202-442-4445, http://dcra.dc.gov/dcra
Hours	Monday–Friday: 8 a.m. to 2 a.m.; Saturday: 8 a.m. to 3 a.m.; Sunday: 10 a.m. to 3 a.m.

FLORIDA	
Dram Shop State?	No
BAC Level	0.08
Age—Pour	18
Age—Sell	18
Age—Serve	18
Happy Hour Laws	May offer food and drink combinations for a special price.
Number of Drinks	Not regulated.
Max Alcohol per Drink	Not regulated.
Mandatory Server Training	No

Notes on Training: Florida does not mandate training, approve programs, or offer a state program. Florida has a Responsible Vendor Act that sets standards for licensees to meet in order to be considered a responsible vendor. Licensees who obtain this status can present it as a mitigating factor against penalties for violations by employees.

Web/Contact for State	Florida Division of Alcoholic Beverages & Tobacco, 850-488-3227, www.state.fl.us/dbpr/abt
Hours	Local option 7 days a week.

GEORGIA, con't	
Dram Shop State?	Yes
BAC Level	0.08
Age—Pour	18
Age—Sell	18
Age—Serve	18
Happy Hour Laws	Regulated by local ordinances.
Number of Drinks	Not regulated.
Max Alcohol per Drink	Not regulated.
Mandatory Server Training	No
Notes on Training: Does not currently regulate server training. However, the State Revenue Department does have a training program for wholesale dealers, retail dealers, and consumption on premises dealers.	
Web/Contact for State	Georgia Alcohol & Tobacco Division, 404-417-4900
Hours	Local communities set laws on hours.

HAWAII	
Dram Shop State?	Yes
BAC Level	0.08
Age—Pour	18
Age—Sell	18
Age—Serve	18
Happy Hour Laws	No free drinks when connected to the sale of other merchandise. Encouraging or promoting any organized game that awards alcohol as a prize or promotes excessive drinking is prohibited. Food and drink combos may be offered as long as the liquor is not used as an inducement. No food with the liquor offered "free" if the food item is purchased. No differentiation between "happy hour," "drink specials" and "promotions." Laws vary by locality; contact county liquor commission for further details.
Number of Drinks	No information available at this time.
Max Alcohol per Drink	No information available at this time.
Mandatory Server Training	Server training regulations are enforced at the local level in Hawaii.
Notes on Training: No information available at this time.	
Web/Contact for State	Liquor Commission of the City and County of Honolulu, 808-523-4458; Hawaii: 808-961-8218; Kauai: 808-241-6580; Maui: 808-243-7753; www.co.honolulu.hi.us/liq

HAWAII, con't	
Hours	Monday–Saturday: 6 a.m. to 2 a.m.; 6 a.m. to 4 a.m. for hotels; 8 a.m. to 4 a.m. for cabarets; Sundays: 6 a.m. to 2 a.m.

IDAHO	
Dram Shop State?	Yes
BAC Level	0.08
Age—Pour	19
Age—Sell	19
Age—Serve	19
Happy Hour Laws	No official "happy hour" laws. May offer a food and drink combo for a special price.
Number of Drinks	Not regulated.
Max Alcohol per Drink	Not regulated.
Mandatory Server Training	No
Notes on Training: Idaho currently does not regulate server training. The ABC does provide a training program for licensees.	
Web/Contact for State	State Liquor Dispensary, 208-947-9400, www2.state.id.us/isld
Hours	On-Premise Drinking: Monday–Saturday: 10 a.m. to 1 a.m. (local ordinances can extend or limit); Sunday: Permitted only through local option.

ILLINOIS	
Dram Shop State?	Yes
BAC Level	0.08
Age—Pour	18 (unless regulated by local ordinance)
Age—Sell	21 (unless regulated by local ordinance)
Age—Serve	18 (unless regulated by local ordinance)
Happy Hour Laws	No single-priced or unlimited-service drink specials. No free drinks or advertise any of the aforementioned practices. May offer a food and drink combo (meal package) for a special price
Number of Drinks	One
Max Alcohol per Drink	Not regulated.
Mandatory Server Training	At local level.
Notes on Training: Local government authorities may enact ordinances with requirements that mandate server-training programs, ranging from who is required to participate to who may provide the training. The Illinois Liquor Control Act states that if BASSET training is mandated, an Illinois BASSET licensee must perform it.	
Web/Contact for State	Illinois Liquor Control Commission, 312-814-2206, www.state.il.us/lcc
Hours	Local option but no liquor sales on Sunday unless provided by local ordinance.

INDIANA	
Dram Shop State?	Yes
BAC Level	0.08
Age—Pour	21
Age—Sell	18 for drug/grocery, 21 everywhere else.
Age—Serve	21
Happy Hour Laws	No two-for-one drink specials. Drink specials must last for the entire business day.
Number of Drinks	No more than one drink per order for one.
Max Alcohol per Drink	Not regulated.
Mandatory Server Training	Yes
Notes on Training: Effective July 1, 2005, all servers, sellers and some managers will be required to receive training. Affected employees will have until July 1, 2008, to complete training	
Web/Contact for State	Alcohol & Tobacco Commission, 317-232-2469, www.in.gov/atc or comments@atc.in.gov
Hours	Monday–Saturday: 7 a.m. to 3 a.m.; Sunday: Noon to 12:30 a.m.

IOWA	
Dram Shop State?	Yes
BAC Level	0.08
Age—Pour	18
Age—Sell	16
Age—Serve	18
Happy Hour Laws	Iowa does not have laws regulating "happy hours" or promotions, but local ordinance may apply. May offer a food and drink combination for a special price. "Happy hour" "drink special" and "promotions" are not regulated.
Number of Drinks	Local ordinance may apply.
Max Alcohol per Drink	Not regulated.
Mandatory Server Training	No
Notes on Training: Iowa currently does not regulate server training, nor does the state provide a training program for licensees. However, server training is recommended.	
Web/Contact for State	Alcoholic Beverages Division, 866-469-2223, www.iowaabd.com
Hours	Monday–Saturday: 6 a.m. to 2 a.m.; Sunday: 8 a.m. to 2 a.m.

KANSAS	
Dram Shop State?	No
BAC Level	0.08
Age—Pour	21 to mix or dispense.
Age—Sell	21
Age—Serve	18 to serve; if no less than 50% of gross receipts are derived from the sale of food, otherwise 21.
Happy Hour Laws	No single-priced, unlimited-service drink specials or free drinks for patrons. May not encourage or promote any organized game that awards alcohol as a prize or promotes excessive drinking. May offer a food and drink combo for a special price dependent upon the licensee being able to articulate how much of that price was for the drink versus the food. The same drink would have to be offered for that same price as a solo purchase for the entire day. Regardless of the terms used, "happy hour," "drink special" and/or "promotion," all drinks have to have the same price throughout the same day/evening.
Number of Drinks	Not regulated.
Max Alcohol per Drink	Not regulated.
Mandatory Server Training	No

KANSAS, con't	
Notes on Training: Kansas currently does not regulate server training; however, the state does provide a training program for licensees who opt to take it in lieu of serving a suspension upon first violation (available only for underage violations).	
Web/Contact for State	Dept. of Revenue, 785-296-7015, www.ksrevenue.org/abc.htm
Hours	Monday–Saturday: 9 a.m. to 2 a.m.; Sunday: 9 a.m. to 2 a.m.

KENTUCKY	
Dram Shop State?	No
BAC Level	0.08
Age—Pour	20
Age—Sell	20
Age—Serve	20
Happy Hour Laws	Licensees may not offer patrons free or complimentary drinks. The law does allow a licensee to offer a food and drink combination for a special price.
Number of Drinks	Not regulated.
Max Alcohol per Drink	Not regulated.
Mandatory Server Training	No
Notes on Training: Kentucky currently does not regulate server training. The state offers a program called STAR that covers Kentucky laws.	
Web/Contact for State	Alcoholic Beverage Control, 502-564-4850, abc.info@ky.gov
Hours	Monday–Saturday: Local option can set hours between 6 a.m. to midnight. Sunday: local ordinance may vote to permit Sunday sales.

LOUISIANA	
Dram Shop State?	No
BAC Level	0.08
Age—Pour	18
Age—Sell	18
Age—Serve	18
Happy Hour Laws	All-you-can-drink limitations. Licensees may offer single-priced, unlimited, drink specials. All-you-can-drink must end before 10 p.m.
Number of Drinks	Not regulated.
Max Alcohol per Drink	Not regulated.
Mandatory Server Training	Yes
Notes on Training: Responsible Vendor Act is mandatory and all servers have to be certified every two years. Some cities do regulate server training and offer their own training.	
Web/Contact for State	Louisiana Office of Alcohol & Tobacco Control, 225-925-4041, www.atc.rev.state.la.us
Hours	Local option; Sunday sales: governed by local ordinance.

MAINE	
Dram Shop State?	Yes
BAC Level	0.08
Age—Pour	17 [Note: All require supervisor on duty who is at least 21.]
Age—Sell	17 [Note: All require supervisor on duty who is at least 21.]
Age—Serve	17 [Note: All require supervisor on duty who is at least 21.]
Happy Hour Laws	No free drinks or encourage or promote any organized game that awards alcohol as a prize or promotes excessive drinking. May offer a food and drink combo for a special price. Maine distinguishes between "happy hour," "drink special" and/or "promotions."
Number of Drinks	Two
Max Alcohol per Drink	Not regulated.
Mandatory Server Training	Yes
Notes on Training: State-established criteria for server training programs, approved courses, and monitored training. Server training not mandatory. The state offers two training programs through its liquor offices.	
Web/Contact for State	Maine Bureau of Alcoholic Beverages, 1-800-452-4663, Ext. 2555, www.maineliquor.com
Hours	Monday–Saturday: 6 a.m. to 1 a.m.; Sundays: 9 a.m. to 1 a.m.

MARYLAND	
Dram Shop State?	No
BAC Level	0.08
Age—Pour	18 for beer/wine licensees, 21 for beer/wine/ liquor licensee.
Age—Sell	18 for beer/light wine, 21 for Class D licensees.
Age—Serve	18 for beer/wine licensees, 21 for beer/wine/ liquor licensees.
Happy Hour Laws	City/County liquor control boards regulate "happy hours" on a local level. All alcohol beverages consumed on a retail premise must be purchased from that retail premise. May restrict free snacks/food during "happy hours."
Number of Drinks	Subject to local regulations.
Max Alcohol per Drink	Varies by city and county; generally not more than 2 oz. per drink; however this is not regulated by the state.
Mandatory Server Training	Yes

Notes on Training: State approves server-training programs. Certification must be completed every four years. A permit is needed for both the program and the trainer. Program providers and trainers must re-register with the state every year by October 31. Retail establishments must have a minimum of one employee trained in a server-training program in order to renew or apply for a new license. The holder of a Statewide Caterer's (SCAT) license shall have at least one individual on-site during a catered event that has been certified by an alcohol-awareness program licensed by the State Comptroller's Office.

MARYLAND, con't	
Web/Contact for State	Comptroller of Maryland, 410-260-7314, www.comp.state.md.us
Hours	Local option on sales time.

MASSACHUSETTS

Dram Shop State?	Yes
BAC Level	0.08
Age—Pour	18
Age—Sell	18
Age—Serve	18
Happy Hour Laws	No offering single-priced, unlimited-service drink specials; free drinks to patrons; encouraging any organized game that awards alcohol as a prize; or promoting excessive drinking.
Number of Drinks	Two
Max Alcohol per Drink	Not regulated.
Mandatory Server Training	No
Notes on Training: None available.	
Web/Contact for State	Massachusetts Alcoholic Beverages Control Commission, 617-727-3040, www.mass.gov/abcc
Hours	On-Premise Drinking: No official hours; Sundays: complex law; local licensing boards may regulate hours. See state statutes.

MICHIGAN	
Dram Shop State?	Yes
BAC Level	0.08
Age—Pour	18
Age—Sell	18
Age—Serve	18
Happy Hour Laws	No offering single-priced, unlimited-service drink specials, free drinks to patrons, or two-for-one drink specials.
Number of Drinks	Not regulated.
Max Alcohol per Drink	Not regulated.
Mandatory Server Training	Yes—under certain circumstances.
Notes on Training: A licensee obtaining a new on-premise license or transferring more than 50% interest in an existing on-premise license is required to have server-trained supervisory personnel employed during all hours alcoholic beverages are served.	
Web/Contact for State	Michigan Liquor Control Commission, 517-322-1345, www.michigan.gov/cis
Hours	Monday–Saturday: 7 a.m. to 2 a.m.; Sunday: Noon to 2 a.m. with Sunday sales permit.

"

MINNESOTA	
Dram Shop State?	Yes
BAC Level	0.1
Age—Pour	18
Age—Sell	18
Age—Serve	Under 17 not permitted to work in areas where alcohol is served or consumed.
Happy Hour Laws	No current statutes/rules governing "happy hours." Rules Chapter 7515/0740(L) does not allow premiums or inducements to encourage alcoholic purchases and consumption. There is a difference between "happy hour," "drink specials" and/or "promotions." "Happy hour" and drink specials for the most part would be considered one and the same. Drink promos may or may not be legal depending on the terms and conditions of the promotion. Recommends that if interested in running drink promos, submit them for review by the state agency.
Number of Drinks	Not regulated.
Max Alcohol per Drink	Not regulated.
Mandatory Server Training	No
Notes on Training: Does not regulate server training, nor does the state provide a training program for licensees.	
Web/Contact for State	Dept. of Public Safety Alcohol & Gambling Enforcement, 651-296-6979, www.dps.state.mn.us

MINNESOTA , con't	
Hours	Monday–Saturday: 8 a.m. to 2 a.m.; Sunday: Noon to 2 a.m.; may restrict on-premises alcohol sales on holidays.

MISSISSIPPI	
Dram Shop State?	Yes
BAC Level	0.08
Age—Pour	21
Age—Sell	21
Age—Serve	18
Happy Hour Laws	No promotion may require proof of purchase of an alcohol beverage. All drinks must be served to the customer. Bottle sales, except for wines and champagnes, are prohibited. Allowance to offer a food and drink combo for a special price.
Number of Drinks	Not regulated.
Max Alcohol per Drink	Not regulated.
Mandatory Server Training	No
Notes on Training: Does not regulate server training, nor do they offer server-training programs through the state. However, a one-hour education program on ABC laws is offered free of charge by ABC Enforcement Agents.	
Web/Contact for State	Office of Alcoholic Beverage Control, 601-856-1301, www.mstc.state.ms.us
Hours	Monday–Saturday: 10 a.m. to midnight; Sunday: prohibited. May be allowed/limited by the commission upon request by local jurisdiction.

MISSOURI	
Dram Shop State?	Yes
BAC Level	0.08
Age—Pour	21
Age—Sell	21; 18 to serve with permission in some establishments.
Age—Serve	18 to serve with permission in some establishments.
Happy Hour Laws	May give free drinks, have two-for-one specials, etc. Prohibited from advertising these specials; allows, under certain conditions, offering of a food and drink combo for a special price.
Number of Drinks	Not regulated.
Max Alcohol per Drink	Not regulated.
Mandatory Server Training	No
Notes on Training: Does not regulate server training. However, a licensee can request a session with an enforcement agent to review the laws and information regarding preventing intoxication and recognizing intoxicated patrons.	
Web/Contact for State	Liquor Control Division, 573-751-2333, www.mdlc.state.mo.us
Hours	Monday–Saturday: 6 a.m. to 1:30 a.m.; Sunday: 9 a.m. to midnight; designated convention site: Monday–Saturday till 3 a.m.

MONTANA	
Dram Shop State?	Yes
BAC Level	0.08
Age—Pour	18
Age—Sell	As allowed by state and federal labor laws.
Age—Serve	As allowed by state and federal labor laws.
Happy Hour Laws	May not sell "liquor" for less than the posted price. No regulations regarding food and drink combos. Promos are considered items such as neck hangers, coupons, rebates, etc. Every promo must have prior approval from the state prior. No definitions in the state statute for "happy hour" and drink specials.
Number of Drinks	Not regulated.
Max Alcohol per Drink	Not regulated.
Mandatory Server Training	No
Notes on Training: Does not regulate server training, nor does the state provide a training program for licensees.	
Web/Contact for State	Montana Liquor Licensing, 406-444-6900, www.mt.gov/revenue/forbusinesses
Hours	Monday–Saturday: 8 a.m. to 2 a.m.; Sunday: 8 a.m. to 2 a.m.; sales may be further restricted by local ordinances.

NEBRASKA	
Dram Shop State?	No
BAC Level	0.08
Age—Pour	19
Age—Sell	19
Age—Serve	19
Happy Hour Laws	May not offer single-priced, unlimited service drink specials or two-for-one drink specials. Allowance to offer a food and drink combo for a special price. Differentiates between "happy hour," "drink specials," and/or "promotions."
Number of Drinks	One
Max Alcohol per Drink	Not regulated.
Mandatory Server Training	No
Notes on Training: Does not regulate server training, nor does the state provide a training program for licensees. Does require training for new license applicants who do not have experience or training in the sales or serving of alcoholic beverages.	
Web/Contact for State	Liquor Control Commission, 402-471-2571, www.nol.org/home/NLCC
Hours	Monday–Saturday: 6 a.m. to 1 a.m.; Sunday: check local ordinances.

NEVADA	
Dram Shop State?	No
BAC Level	0.08
Age—Pour	Regulated at the city and county level.
Age—Sell	Regulated at the city and county level.
Age—Serve	Regulated at the city and county level.
Happy Hour Laws	"Happy hour" laws vary by city and county. Contact local agency for further information.
Number of Drinks	Regulated at the city and county level.
Max Alcohol per Drink	Regulated at the city and county level.
Mandatory Server Training	A new statewide mandatory training law will become effective on July 1, 2007. Las Vegas and Clark County have mandatory training ordinances. Reno has a limited training ordinance for sellers, mandatory for only a part of downtown Reno.
Notes on Training: Training for sellers, servers and security staff in Nevada will become mandatory statewide on July 1, 2007. Regulations have not yet been drafted. Currently Clark County and Las Vegas have mandatory training ordinances. Reno has a limited training ordinance, mandatory only for a part of downtown Reno.	
Web/Contact for State	Dept. of Taxation, 775-684-2000, tax.state.nv.us
Hours	Regulated by local governments only.

NEW HAMPSHIRE	
Dram Shop State?	Yes
BAC Level	0.08
Age—Pour	18
Age—Sell	16 to run a register in an off-premise situation (with 18-year-old supervision).
Age—Serve	18
Happy Hour Laws	No free drinks to patrons. No special drink prices may be advertised off the licensed premises. per RSA 179.42, may offer a food and drink combo for a special price.
Number of Drinks	No more than one drink in the food/drink combo.
Max Alcohol per Drink	Not regulated.
Mandatory Server Training	Yes—under certain circumstances.
Notes on Training: It is mandatory for any new licensee or his/her designee to attend a management training seminar, developed and provided by the State Liquor Commission within 45 days of issuance of the license. This requirement applies to both on-premise and off-premise licensees. This requirement does not apply to anyone holding a license as of the effective date (September 9, 2001).	
Web/Contact for State	State Liquor Commission, 603-271-3134, info@liquor.state.nh.us
Hours	Monday–Saturday: 6 a.m. to 1 a.m.; Sunday: 6 a.m. to 1 a.m.

NEW JERSEY	
Dram Shop State?	Yes
BAC Level	0.08
Age—Pour	18
Age—Sell	18
Age—Serve	18
Happy Hour Laws	No single-priced, unlimited-service or two-for-one drink specials. May not encourage or promote any organized game that awards alcohol as a prize or promotes excessive drinking. Allowance to offer a food and drink combo for a special price.
Number of Drinks	Not regulated.
Max Alcohol per Drink	Not regulated.
Mandatory Server Training	No
Notes on Training: New Jersey currently does not regulate server training.	
Web/Contact for State	Division of Alcoholic Beverage Control, 609-984-2830, www.state.nj.us/lps/abc/index.html
Hours	Determined by city ordinance.

NEW MEXICO	
Dram Shop State?	Yes
BAC Level	0.08
Age—Pour	21
Age—Sell	19 (in an establishment where the primary source of revenue is food.)
Age—Serve	19 (in an establishment where the primary source of revenue is food.)
Happy Hour Laws	No single-priced, unlimited service, free drinks for patrons or two-for-one drink specials.
Number of Drinks	Two
Max Alcohol per Drink	Not regulated.
Mandatory Server Training	Yes
Notes on Training: State certification program using state-provided curriculum.	
Web/Contact for State	Alcohol and Gaming Division, 505-476-4875, rld.state.nm.us
Hours	Monday–Saturday: 7 a.m. to 2 a.m.; Sunday: Noon to midnight (Sunday sales permit required).

NEW YORK	
Dram Shop State?	Yes
BAC Level	0.08
Age—Pour	18
Age—Sell	18
Age—Serve	18
Happy Hour Laws	No unlimited drink offerings; for example, "all you can drink."
Number of Drinks	Not regulated.
Max Alcohol per Drink	Not regulated.
Mandatory Server Training	No
Notes on Training: A voluntary Responsible Vendor Program sets standards in order to be considered a responsible vendor. Status can be presented as a mitigating factor against penalties for violations by employees. Consult the New York State Liquor Authority for more details.	
Web/Contact for State	Division of Alcoholic Beverage Control, 518-474-0810, www.abc.state.ny.us
Hours	Monday–Saturday: 8 a.m. to midnight. Differs by county.

NORTH CAROLINA	
Dram Shop State?	Yes
BAC Level	0.08
Age—Pour	21 to pour distilled spirits, 18 to pour beer and wine.
Age—Sell	18
Age—Serve	18
Happy Hour Laws	"Happy hours" or drink specials must be offered for the entire business day. No free drinks or offer two-for-one drink specials. No allowance to offer a food and drink combo for a special price. No difference between "happy hour," "drink specials" and/or "promotions."
Number of Drinks	One
Max Alcohol per Drink	Not regulated.
Mandatory Server Training	No, but ABC provides free Responsible Alcohol Seller Program training provided by their education specialists.
Notes on Training: Does not regulate server training. However, does offer the BARS program (Be A Responsible Server), taught by alcohol law enforcement agents. BARS is a one- to two-hour program and is provided at no cost to the retailer.	
Web/Contact for State	Alcoholic Beverage Commission, 919-779-0700, www.ncabc.com or ContactUs@ncabc.com
Hours	Monday–Saturday: 7 a.m. to 2 a.m.; Sunday: Noon to 2 a.m. with a mixed beverage or brown bagging permit. Election Day: no restrictions.

NORTH DAKOTA	
Dram Shop State?	Yes
BAC Level	0.08
Age—Pour	21
Age—Sell	19 to collect money (see "Serve" conditions below)
Age—Serve	19 to serve, if: in dining area separate from bar and gross food sales are at least equal to gross alcohol sales and done under direct supervision of someone 21 or older.
Happy Hour Laws	Subject to local regulations.
Number of Drinks	Not regulated.
Max Alcohol per Drink	Not regulated.
Mandatory Server Training	No
Notes on Training: None available	
Web/Contact for State	Office of the State Tax Commissioner, 701-328-4576, www.wineinstitute.org /shipwine/state_abcz/abcz.htm#mstates
Hours	Monday–Saturday: 8 a.m. to 1 a.m.; Sunday: Noon to 1 a.m.

OHIO	
Dram Shop State?	Yes
BAC Level	0.08
Age—Pour	21 to serve liquor across the bar, 19 to serve beer and wine across the bar.
Age—Sell	19 as server, 21 to sell across the bar.
Age—Serve	19
Happy Hour Laws	No single-priced, unlimited-service, free drinks for patrons or two-for-one drink specials. May not encourage or promote any organized game that awards alcohol as a prize or promotes excessive drinking. "Happy hour" drink specials must end before 9 p.m.
Number of Drinks	Not regulated.
Max Alcohol per Drink	Not regulated.
Mandatory Server Training	No
Notes on Training: No. The Department of Public Safety offers a server education program to retail permit holders. Call 614-644-2415 for details.	
Web/Contact for State	Div. of Liquor Control, 614-644-2411, www.liquorcontrol.ohio.gov/liquor.htm
Hours	Monday–Saturday: 5:30 a.m. to 1 a.m.; Nightclubs: 5:30 a.m. to 2:30 a.m.; Sunday sales permit required: 11 a.m., 1 p.m., or 10 a.m. to midnight based on local option.

OKLAHOMA	
Dram Shop State?	No
BAC Level	0.08
Age—Pour	21
Age—Sell	21
Age—Serve	18, if server works outside separate bar area.
Happy Hour Laws	No difference between "happy hour," "drink specials" and "promotions." "Happy hours" are illegal—no reduced drink prices. Drink specials must occur for an entire calendar week (Sunday–Saturday). Promos are allowed if they follow the same calendar week schedule. No allowance to offer a food and drink combo for a special price.
Number of Drinks	Two
Max Alcohol per Drink	Not regulated.
Mandatory Server Training	No
Notes on Training: None available.	
Web/Contact for State	ABLE Commission, 405-521-3484, www.able.state.ok.us
Hours	Monday–Saturday: 10 a.m. to 2 a.m.; set by county. Sundays: check local ordinances.

OREGON	
Dram Shop State?	Yes
BAC Level	0.08
Age—Pour	18 with a service permit, restrictions apply to 18–20 year olds.
Age—Sell	18
Age—Serve	18 with a service permit, restrictions apply to 18–20 year olds.
Happy Hour Laws	May not be advertised outside the licensed business. Same rule applies to a licensee who wishes to offer a food and drink combo for a special price if the price includes a temporary price reduction on the alcohol. Does not distinguish between "happy hour," "drink specials," and/or "promotions."
Number of Drinks	Not regulated.
Max Alcohol per Drink	Not regulated.
Mandatory Server Training	Yes
Notes on Training: There is a mandatory alcohol server education program managed by the Oregon Liquor Control Commission (OLCC). It is for owners, managers, and servers of alcohol at businesses licensed for on-premises consumption.	
Web/Contact for State	Liquor Control Commission, 800-452-6522, 503-872-5000, www.olcc.state.or.us
Hours	Monday–Saturday 7 a.m. to 2:30 a.m.; Sunday: 7 a.m. to 2:30 a.m.

PENNSYLVANIA	
Dram Shop State?	Yes
BAC Level	0.08
Age—Pour	18
Age—Sell	18
Age—Serve	18
Happy Hour Laws	May not offer single-priced, unlimited service or two-for-one drink specials. "Happy hour" specials may only be two consecutive hours long and must occur before 12:00 a.m. Drinks of an increased size must be accompanied by a corresponding increased price. One daily drink special may be offered so long as it ends by 12 a.m. Does allow offering of a food and drink combo for a special price so long as it does not violate Section 13.102 of the Board's Regulations on the licensee's ability to discount the price of alcoholic beverages.
Number of Drinks	Unlimited as long as there is no discount for multiple purchases and the person is not visibly intoxicated.
Max Alcohol per Drink	Not regulated.
Mandatory Server Training	No

PENNSYLVANIA , con't

Notes on Training: No required server training. However, the state does offer a voluntary "Responsible Alcohol Management Program" (RAMP). Licensees' compliance with the Responsible Alcohol Management provisions can be a mitigating factor in a subsequent citation for sales to minors or visibly intoxicated persons. While the program is otherwise voluntary, a judge may order a licensee to comply with the Responsible Alcohol Management provisions for up to a year, if the licensee has been found to have sold alcohol to minors or to a visibly intoxicated person.

Web/Contact for State	Liquor Control Board, 717-783-9454, www.lcb.state.pa.us
Hours	Monday–Saturday: 7 a.m. to 2 a.m.; Sunday: 11 a.m. to 2 a.m. (with permit).

RHODE ISLAND	
Dram Shop State?	Yes
BAC Level	0.08
Age—Pour	18
Age—Sell	18
Age—Serve	18
Happy Hour Laws	May not offer single-priced, unlimited-service or encourage or promote any organized game which awards alcohol as a prize or promotes excessive drinking.
Number of Drinks	One
Max Alcohol per Drink	1.0 to 1.5 oz.
Mandatory Server Training	Yes
Notes on Training: The law became effective January 1, 2006.	
Web/Contact for State	Department of Business Regulation, Liquor Control Administration, 401-222-2562, www.dbr.state.ri.us/liquor_comp.html
Hours	Monday–Saturday: 6 a.m. to 1 a.m.; Sunday: 6 a.m. to 1 a.m.

SOUTH CAROLINA	
Dram Shop State?	Yes
BAC Level	0.08
Age—Pour	21
Age—Sell	No minimum age if sold in sealed containers.
Age—Serve	18
Happy Hour Laws	No two-or-more-for-the-price-of-one drink specials and may not give free mixed drinks, beer, or wine. Regular drink prices may be reduced between 4:00 p.m. and 8:00 p.m. only. The State General Assembly will issue new regulation for the use of standard-sized bottles during the 2005 legislative session.
Number of Drinks	Not regulated.
Max Alcohol per Drink	Not regulated.
Mandatory Server Training	Yes
Notes on Training: Server training is voluntary.	
Web/Contact for State	Dept. of Revenue & Taxation, 803-898-5864, www.sctax.org/default.htm
Hours	Monday–Saturday: 24 hours for beer and wine, 10 a.m. to 2 a.m. for liquor, cease at midnight Saturdays; Sunday: local option.

SOUTH DAKOTA	
Dram Shop State?	No
BAC Level	0.08
Age—Pour	21
Age—Sell	If 50% of retail is transacted from the sale of food, persons 18–20 may wait tables, no bartending.
Age—Serve	If 50% of retail is transacted from the sale of food, persons 18–20 may wait tables, no bartending.
Happy Hour Laws	Does not specifically address "happy hour." May offer a food and drink combo for a special price under the circumstances that the licensee cannot sell below wholesale cost (drink). No difference between "happy hour," "drink specials," and/or "promotion," as the statute only refers to selling below wholesale cost.
Number of Drinks	Not regulated.
Max Alcohol per Drink	Not regulated.
Mandatory Server Training	No
Mandatory Topics, language or questions	Yes

Notes on Training: Done on a voluntary basis. Approved training cuts civil penalties in half for licensees whose clerks sell alcohol to teenagers

SOUTH DAKOTA , con't	
Web/Contact for State	Dept. of Revenue & Regulation, 605-773-3311, www.state.sd.us/drr2/revenue.html
Hours	On-Premise Drinking: Monday–Saturday: 7 a.m. to 2 a.m.; Sunday: if granted Sunday sales by local option—11 a.m. to midnight; local ordinances may be stricter.

TENNESSEE	
Dram Shop State?	Yes
BAC Level	0.08
Age—Pour	18
Age—Sell	18
Age—Serve	18
Happy Hour Laws	May not offer single-priced, unlimited service, give free drinks to patrons, or encourage or promote any organized game that awards alcohol as a prize or promotes excessive drinking. May not offer "happy hour" specials after 10 p.m.
Number of Drinks	No limit until 10 p.m., then one drink at a time.
Max Alcohol per Drink	Not regulated.
Mandatory Server Training	Yes
Notes on Training: Regulating law established May 1995 (effective July 1996.) Does not apply to beer-only establishments. They are regulated by county beer boards. Employees in establishments regulated by beer boards are not required to have state server permits.	
Web/Contact for State	Alcoholic Beverage Commission, 615-741-1602, www.state.tn.us/abc
Hours	Monday–Saturday: 8 a.m. to 3 a.m.; Sunday: 10 a.m. to 3 a.m.; unless municipality has opted out; if so, noon to 3 a.m.

TEXAS	
Dram Shop State?	Yes
BAC Level	0.08
Age—Pour	18
Age—Sell	18
Age—Serve	18
Happy Hour Laws	No single-priced, unlimited service or two-for-one drink specials. May not encourage or promote any organized game that awards alcohol as a prize or promotes excessive drinking. "Happy hour" specials must end before 11:00 p.m. May offer a food and drink combo for a special price. No difference in the law between "happy hour," "drink specials" and "promotions."
Number of Drinks	Two
Max Alcohol per Drink	Not regulated.
Mandatory Server Training	Yes

Notes on Training: Has laws regulating server training for all people who sell, serve, dispense, or deliver alcohol. They establish which entities are eligible as providers for the training and set the minimum requirements for a training curriculum. The Texas Alcoholic Beverage Commission offers the Stop Alcohol Violations Early (SAVE) program, developed by the commission for retailers at no cost. Program is approximately one hour in length and discusses the laws concerning sales to minors, intoxicated customers, the consequences of such illegal sales, and regulatory matters. SAVE does not meet the requirements for seller/server certification.

TEXAS, con't	
Web/Contact for State	Alcoholic Beverage Commission, 1-888-THE-TABC, 512-206-3333, www.tabc.state.tx.us
Hours	Monday–Saturday: 7 a.m. to midnight—late-hours permit/license available in certain areas extends hours of sale to 2 a.m.; Sunday: with food service or at a "sporting venue" may start at 10 a.m. to midnight. Other permits may start at noon and serve until 2 a.m. with late-hours permit.

UTAH	
Dram Shop State?	Yes
BAC Level	0.08
Age—Pour	21
Age—Sell	21
Age—Serve	21
Happy Hour Laws	Prohibited from engaging in discounting practices that encourage over-consumption of alcohol (for example, "happy hours," "two-for-ones," "all you can drink" for a set price, free alcohol, selling at less than cost, etc.). May not buy a patron a drink. Ads may not encourage over-consumption or intoxication, promote the intoxicating effects of alcohol, or overtly promote increased consumption of alcoholic products. No food and drink combos for a special price.
Number of Drinks	Patrons of restaurants may have no more than one spirituous liquor beverage before them at a time. Patrons of restaurants, limited restaurants, and private clubs may have no more than two alcoholic beverages (of any kind) before them at a time.
Max Alcohol per Drink	1 oz. of primary liquor per drink. Beer may be sold to an individual patron only in a container that does not exceed 1 liter. Beer may be sold by the pitcher (up to 2 liters) to two or more patrons.
Mandatory Server Training	Yes

UTAH, con't

Notes on Training: Required server training for all who sell or furnish alcoholic beverages for consumption on the premises. Employees, including managers and supervisors, are required to be server trained within 30 days of hire. The state has approved training programs to be provided by private entities. Trainers are required to register each server who successfully completes their course with the state.

Web/Contact for State	Dept. of Alcoholic Beverage Control, 801-977-6800, hotline@utah.gov or www.alcbev.state.ut.us
Hours	Monday–Saturday: 10 a.m. to 1 a.m.; Sunday: 10 a.m. to 1 a.m.

VERMONT	
Dram Shop State?	Yes
BAC Level	0.08
Age—Pour	18
Age—Sell	16 for off-premise, 18 for on-premise
Age—Serve	18
Happy Hour Laws	No alcohol at reduced prices for any period less than a full day. Cannot encourage or promote any organized game that awards alcohol as a prize or promotes excessive drinking. May allow food and drink combination for a special price as long as they do not use the words "complimentary" or "free."
Number of Drinks	Two
Max Alcohol per Drink	32 oz. of beer; 4 oz. of spirits
Mandatory Server Training	Yes

Notes on Training: Requires all licensees (both on- and off-premise) to complete a Licensee Education and Server training course. Offers a four-hour course called ASAP (Alcohol Servers Awareness Program) at no cost to the retailer. Recertification is required every three years or licenses will not be renewed and no new license will be issued without training. Employees are required to be trained before they can sell or serve alcohol. Can be done by either attending a seminar put on by the DLC or trained by their employer using materials provided by the DLC. Employees must be trained once every two years.

Web/Contact for State	Dept. of Liquor Control, 802-828-2345, www.state.vt.us/dlc

VERMONT, con't	
Hours	Monday–Saturday: 8 a.m. 2 a.m.;
	Sunday: 8 a.m. to 2 a.m.

VIRGINIA	
Dram Shop State?	No
BAC Level	0.08
Age—Pour	21
Age—Sell	18
Age—Serve	18
Happy Hour Laws	No single-priced, unlimited service, free drinks for patrons or two-for-one drink specials. The hours that "happy hour" can be conducted are from 6 a.m. to 9 p.m. No "happy hour" drink specials between 9 p.m. and 2 a.m. of the following day. Cannot advertise "happy hour" in the media or on the exterior of the premises. Cannot increase the amount of the alcoholic beverages in a drink without charging a higher price. Cannot sell pitchers of mixed beverages.
Number of Drinks	Two
Max Alcohol per Drink	Not more than 24 oz per drink; cannot serve one customer an entire bottle of spirits
Mandatory Server Training	No
Notes on Training: Does not regulate server training. However, ABC agents provide both trainer workshops and server sessions throughout the state.	
Web/Contact for State	Dept. of Alcoholic Beverage Control, 804-213-4400, www.abc.state.va.us
Hours	Monday–Saturday: 6 a.m. to 2 a.m.; Sunday: 6 a.m. to 2 a.m.

WASHINGTON	
Dram Shop State?	No
BAC Level	0.08
Age—Pour	21
Age—Sell	18
Age—Serve	18
Happy Hour Laws	No two-for-one drink specials or encourage any activity that promotes excessive drinking. May offer a food and drink combo for a special price as long as no liquor is sold below the cost of acquisition. The law differentiates between "happy hour," "drink specials," and/or "promotions." "Happy hour" is a specific time of day; drink specials can be by house policy but cannot be sold below cost of acquisition; promotions must be approved by the Advertising Coordinator at the LCB. The board can take action against any licensee who promotes over-consumption or consumption by persons under 21.
Number of Drinks	Not regulated.
Max Alcohol per Drink	Not regulated.
Mandatory Server Training	Yes

WASHINGTON , con't

Notes on Training: Mandatory server training program for on-premise establishments became effective January 1, 1997. Requires servers to have either a Class 12 or Class 13 permit. Permits are valid for five years. A list of approved programs and trainers is available from the liquor control board. As of January 1, 2005, trainers must use the standardized exam.

Web/Contact for State	State Liquor Control Board, 360-664-1600, wslcb@liq.wa.gov or www.liq.wa.gov/default.asp
Hours	Monday–Saturday: 6 a.m. to 2 a.m.; Sunday: 6 a.m. to 2 a.m.

WEST VIRGINIA	
Dram Shop State?	No
BAC Level	0.08
Age—Pour	18 (supervised by person over 21 at all times).
Age—Sell	18
Age—Serve	18
Happy Hour Laws	Not covered by West Virginia law.
Number of Drinks	Not regulated.
Max Alcohol per Drink	Not regulated.
Mandatory Server Training	No
Notes on Training: Not regulated.	
Web/Contact for State	Alcohol Beverage Control Administration, 800-642-8208, www.wvabca.com
Hours	Monday–Saturday: 7 a.m. to 3:30 a.m.; Sunday: Noon to 3 a.m.

WISCONSIN	
Dram Shop State?	No
BAC Level	0.08
Age—Pour	18
Age—Sell	18
Age—Serve	18
Happy Hour Laws	No laws specifically addressing "happy hours" or promotions. Does not address whether a licensee is allowed to offer food and drink combos for a special price; therefore, it is permitted. No differentiation between "happy hour," "drink specials" and/or "promotions."
Number of Drinks	Not regulated.
Max Alcohol per Drink	Not regulated.
Mandatory Server Training	Yes
Notes on Training: Requires licensees and servers to obtain alcohol awareness training if they are licensed to have a job selling or serving alcoholic beverages and the city or county requires a permit. In such cases, training is mandatory as a condition of obtaining a license.	
Web/Contact for State	Dept. of Revenue, 608-266-3969, www.dor.state.wi.us
Hours	On-Premise Drinking: Monday–Friday: 6 a.m. to 2 a.m.; Saturday–Sunday: 6 a.m. to 2:30 a.m.

WYOMING	
Dram Shop State?	Yes, with qualifications
BAC Level	0.08
Age—Pour	18
Age—Sell	18
Age—Serve	21 (18 in dining-only areas)
Happy Hour Laws	No laws specifically addressing "happy hours" or promotions. Allows offering of food and drink combs for a special price.
Number of Drinks	Not regulated.
Max Alcohol per Drink	Not regulated.
Mandatory Server Training	Yes
Notes on Training: Has a Voluntary Responsible Vendor Program. The Wyoming Department of Revenue Liquor Division must approve all alcohol server-training programs. All providers (trainers) must be certified per rules and regulations. Training is mandatory in Cheyenne for all servers, on-site managers, and staff involved in "physical security" (bouncers, doorkeepers, etc.). Training is mandatory in Douglas for all owners, managers, and supervisory personnel.	
Web/Contact for State	Dept. of Revenue, 307-777-7961, revenue.state.wy.us
Hours	Monday–Saturday: 6 a.m. to 2 a.m. (maximum); Sunday: 6 a.m. to 2 a.m. (maximum); Note: Municipalities may be more restrictive on Sunday hours.

GLOSSARY

A

AGE Used as a measure of quality with alcohol.

ALCOHOL A colorless, intoxicating liquid produced by distilling fermented fruits, vegetables, and grains.

ALE Alcoholic beverage brewed from top-fermenting yeast.

APERITIF An alcoholic drink taken before a meal to stimulate the appetite.

B

BAC Blood alcohol content.

BACK BAR The area that holds the liquor behind the bar.

BAR ACCESSORIES Any item that is used in a bar.

BAR BACK A bartender's assistant who does not serve drinks.

BAR BOTTLES A decorative bottle intended to be refilled for dispensing various types of liquor.

BEER An alcoholic beverage brewed from a mash of malted barley and other cereals, flavored with hops and fermented with yeast.

BITTERS Alcohol flavored with bitter herbs and roots.

C

CALL Liquor that a

customer specifically asks for by name.

CARAFE A pot or bottle used for serving water, coffee, or wine.

CARBON DIOXIDE A byproduct of fermentation that causes carbonation.

CASK Barrel-shaped container used to store beer or wine.

CHASER A beverage usually drunk immediately after drinking a straight shot of liquor.

COCKTAIL Any alcoholic beverage that mixes two or more ingredients.

COMPS Management-authorized free drinks; complimentary drinks.

CONDITIONING TANK A tank where the beer matures, clarifies, and is naturally carbonated through secondary fermentation.

CONVERTIBLE BAR Open or folding bar.

D

DISTILLATION Purifying liquids through boiling so that the steam or vapors condense to a pure form.

DRAFT Keg beer served on tap.

E

ESTER Compound formed during fermentation giving beer a spicy or fruity taste.

F

FERMENTATION Changing sugars into ethyl alcohol and carbon dioxide.

FERMENTER A closed and sterile container used for fermentation.

FRAPPES The combination of different liquors served over crushed ice; usually an after-dinner drink.

FREE POUR Pouring alcohol without using a measuring device.

G

GRENADINE Nonalcoholic syrup used to sweeten and color drinks.

GUN Used to measure and pour soda.

H

HAND PUMP Used to serve draft beer.

HIGHBALLS A simple mixture of whiskey and club soda served in a tall glass.

HOPS Flowers used to flavor beer and ale.

J

JIGGER Used to calculate an exact amount of liquid; also called a shot glass.

K

KEG One-half barrel that holds approximately 15.5 gallons.

L

LAGER Beer produced with bottom-fermenting yeast; fermented at much colder temperatures than top-fermented beers.

LIGHT BEER Low-calorie beer, also usually low alcohol content.

LIGHT-STRUCK Having a skunk-like smell due to light exposure.

LIQUEUR Alcoholic beverage with a sweet taste made by flavored ingredients and a spirit.

M

MALT LIQUOR Higher alcohol content than standard beer.

METALLIC Over-aged beer.

MIST Filling a glass with crushed ice and then pouring undiluted spirits on top.

MUSTY Moldy flavor and aroma due to cork or brew spillage.

N

NEAT A drink without ice, water, or mixers.

NIGHTCAP A drink taken at the end of an evening.

NONALCOHOLIC A beverage containing less than 0.5 percent alcohol by volume.

O

ON THE ROCKS Alcohol poured over ice cubes.

P

PAR LEVEL Inventory level set to prevent running out of something.

PAR STOCK The inventory available to bartenders without going to the storeroom.

POURING COST The cost determined by dividing consumption by sales.

PROOF Measures the strength of alcohol, expressed by a number that is twice the percentage by volume of alcohol.

R

RACKING Siphoning off the liquid from one vessel to another, leaving behind the sediment on the bottom.

S

SHOT A small amount of liquor; usually one to two ounces.

T

TOP SHELF Liquor that is the most expensive.

TOT Liquor in small amounts.

V

VIRGIN Nonalcoholic drink.

W

WELL House liquor.

REFERENCES

To research this book, I spent time finding books and articles in such diverse disciplines as law, medicine, social sciences, and business. Finding information that was pertinent, precise, and unbiased was a challenge. As a place where people drink, the hospitality industry is often caught in the crossfire between groups who want to prohibit all alcohol and other groups who want it heavily regulated.

When I found material, I used the following criteria for including it in the book:

1. Did it come from a recognized entity within the discipline? Was it regarded by practitioners in that field as being trustworthy?

2. If it was from a published source such as an article or book, had it undergone a peer review process within that field, and had others cited the conclusions as being noteworthy?

3. If it was a research-based piece, was the sample size and composition large enough to make it statistically valid? Did they include details on how they collected and analyzed the data for their report?

If this information was not present, I considered the results preliminary and did not include them within this book. If the data or conclusions were based upon one bar, or one server, I did not include those results in the text. Finally, no matter how high the response rate was, samples based on customers or servers self-responding were also excluded, as those studies had not been successfully replicated. While data based on one server, bar, or a group in a particular area may show promise, a look at the wide variety of laws in the Appendix shows what happens in one locale may not be applicable in another area.

4. If the piece had an overtly anti-bar bias, then it was not included in the research.

As a result, Section II — Management Responsibilities When Serving Alcohol has documentation for each suggestion and strategy within that section. Section III was based on Section II plus the addition of the author's extensive teaching and training experience. References are listed on the following pages; more information is available upon request from the publisher and author.

Finally, a request to fellow researchers in the social sciences, especially those looking for a thesis or dissertation topic: It has been more than 20 years since the last studies of customer behavior in a bar have been published. Except for the work from Kathryn Graham that focuses more on violence rather than drinking per se, not much has been scientifically researched as to the physical surroundings affecting alcohol consumption: such items as music beat, lighting, comfort in seating, or the presence of pool tables. Even twenty years ago, most of that research was preliminary at best. Research in this area would go a long way in helping to understand why people drink under certain conditions.

The following people graciously allowed me to pick their brains and helped me find references on serving alcohol and drinking rates. Dr. Kathryn Graham, of the University of Western Ontario, helped me to find the research that is the foundation of Section II. Mr. Jim Mosher, Director of the Center for the Study of Law Enforcement and Policy, was the first person who helped me to find some older references on customer behavior. Mr. Robert Slatz, Senior Researcher of the Prevention Research Center, explained some of his findings and pointed me in the direction of material for Section II. For the medical section, Susie Peschl, of Aurora Medical, and Dr. Steve Schwimmer, of Kenosha, reviewed the medical chapter for accuracy. Janet Killarney of Boston Hospital and Bernie Killarney of Boston Hospital also read this section and contributed to its creation. For the law chapter, Nathan J. Breen, Esq. of Howe & Hutton, Ltd. law firm reviewed that section with an eye toward its legal foundations. Cheryl Gruise of Kauai Community College helped with Hawaiian Laws, and Mike Mosher of the Wyoming State liquor Association helped find well-hidden legal codes in his state. Lori Stucker was invaluable with her help in creating the Appendix. Steve Armstrong, owner of Chef at Your Door, read the second and third sections with an experienced industry eye.

As always, laws and customs in this area can change quickly. The information in this book is considered reliable as of the publication date, but to make sure, check with competent local legal advice for details.

BOOKS

Hospitality Law: Managerial Legal Issues in the Hospitality Industry, by Stephen Barth. Published by Wiley and Sons, 2001.

The Intervention Handbook: The Legal Aspects of Serving Alcohol Second Edition, by Robert Plotkin. Published by P.S.D. Publishing, 1990.

The Instant Trainer, by C. Leslie Charles and Chris Clarke-Epstein. Published by McGraw-Hill, 1998.

Professional Guide to Alcoholic Beverages, by Robert Lipinski and Kathleen Lipinski. Published by Van Nostrand Reinhold, 1989.

Responsible Beverage Service: An Implementation Handbook for Communities, by James Mosher. Published by Health Promotion Resource Center, 1991.

Restaurant Management, by Nancy Scanlon. Published by Van Nostrand Reinhold, 1993.

Wine and Beverage Standards, by Donald Bell. Published by Van Nostrand Reinhold, 1989.

ARTICLES

Affairs of States: Federal Mandates Won't Solve Age-Old Social Issue of Alcohol Abuse, by Fred G. Sampson. Published in *Nation's Restaurant News New York*: Aug 20, 2001. Vol. 35, Iss. 34, p. 38-40.

Alcohol Lawsuits Seek to Swat Sports Concessionaires for Service at Games, by Paul King. Published in *Nation's Restaurant News New York*: Oct 27, 2003. Vol. 37, Iss. 43, p. 4, 89.

The Emergence of Civil Liability for Dispensing Alcohol: A Comparative Study, Review of Litigation, by Daphne D. Sipes. Published in *University of Texas Law School Publications*, 1988.

Emerging Adult's Substance Use and Risky Behaviors in Club Settings, by Brenda Miller, Debra Furr-Holden, Robert Voas, and Kristen Bright. Published in *Journal of Drug Issues*, Spring 2005, No. 35 (2), p. 357-378.

Health Risks and Benefits of Alcohol Consumption. Published in *Alcohol Research & Health*, Vol 24, No. 1, 2000.

High-Risk Drinking Settings: The Association of Serving and Promotional

Practices with Harmful Drinking, by Tim Stockwell, Ernie Lang, and Phil Rydon. Published in *Addiction*, 1993, No. 88, p. 1519-1526.

Industry Remains Sober in Wake of Alcohol Tragedies, by Carolyn Walkup. Published in *Nation's Restaurant News New York*: Sep 22, 2003, Vol. 37, Iss. 38, p. 134-138.

The Influence of Time, Gender and Group Size on Heavy Drinking in Public Bars, by Richard Sykes and Richard Rowley. Published in *Journal of Studies on Alcohol*, Mar 93, No. 54 (2), p. 133-139.

The Keys to Responsibility, by Miller Beer. Self-published, accessed at their Web site at **www.millerbrewing.com**.

Levels of Drunkenness of Customers Leaving Licensed Premises in Perth, Western Australia: A Comparison of High and Low 'Risk' Premises, by Tim Stockwell, Phil Rydon, Sonia Gianatti, Evan Jenkins, Claudia Ovenden, and David Syed. Published in *British Journal of Addiction*, Jun 1992, No. 87 (6), p. 873-882.

Lee V. Kiku Restaurant: Allocation of Fault Between an Alcohol Vendor and a Patron — What Could Happen After Providing "One More for the Road," by Pamela A. Moore. Published in *American Journal of Trial Advocacy,* Summer 1993.

Missouri Dram Shop Law: Its History and New Direction, by Anthony L. Roberts. Published in *Journal of the Missouri Bar*, Sept-Oct 2003.

Operators That Require Alcoholic-Beverage Training for Workers See Payoff in Protection, by Robin Lee Allen, Alan Gould, Ellen Koteff, Richard Martin, et al. Published in *Nation's Restaurant News New York*: Feb 7, 2005. Vol. 39, Iss. 6, p. 21.

Prevalence of Responsible Hospitality Policies in Licensed Premises That Are Associated with Alcohol-Related Harm, by Justine Daly, Elizabeth Campbell, John Wiggers, and Robyn Considine. Published in *Drug & Alcohol Review*, Jun 2002, Vol. 21 Issue 2, p. 113-121.

Preventive Interventions for On-Premise Drinking: A Promising by Underresearched Area of Prevention, by Kathryn Graham. Published in *Contemporary Drug Problems*, Fall 2000, No. 27, p. 593-668.

Public Drinking Then and Now, by Kathryn Graham. Published in *Contemporary Drug Problems*, Spring 2005, No. 32, p. 45-56.

Qualitative Assessment of Training Programs for Alcohol Servers and Establishment Managers, by Traci Toomey, Gudrun Kilian, John Gehan, Cheryl Perry, Rhonda Jones-Webb, and Alexander Wagnaar.

Published in *Public Health Reports*, March/April 1998, Vol. 113, p. 162-169.

Recalling Prohibition Best Way for Operators to Halt Progress of Anti-Alcohol Campaigns, by Rick Berman. Published in *Nation's Restaurant News New York*: May 24, 2004. Vol. 38, Iss. 21, p. 38, 172-173.

Restaurateurs Still Are Spinning Their Wheels as the BAC Express Continues to Chug Along, by Fred G. Sampson. Published in *Nation's Restaurant News New York*: Feb 16, 2004. Vol. 38, Iss. 7, p. 36-38.

Should Alcohol Consumption Measures Be Adjusted for Gender Differences?, by Kathryn Graham, Richard Wilsnack, Deborah Dawson, and Nancy Vogeltanz. Published in *Addiction*, 1998, No. 93 (8), p. 1137-1147.

Situational Norms for Drinking and Drunkenness: Trends in the U.S. Adult Population, 1979-1990, by Thomas Greenfield and Robin Room. Published in *Addiction*, Jan 1997, No. 92 (1).

The Yin and Yang of Alcohol Intoxication: Implications for Research on the Social Consequences of Drinking, by Kathryn Graham. Published in *Addiction*, Aug 2003, No. 98 (8), p. 1021-1023.

$105M Verdict vs. Aramark Makes Operators Rethink Methods for Training Workers Who Sell Alcohol, by Paul King. Published in *Nation's Restaurant News New York*: Feb 7, 2005. Vol. 39, Iss. 6, p. 1, 64.

WEBPAGES

American Beverage Association
www.abanet.org

American Medical Association
www.ama-assn.org

Mothers Against Drunk Driving (MADD)
www.madd.org

National Institute of Alcohol Abuse and Alcoholism
www.niaaa.nih.gov

National Restaurant Association
www.restaurant.org

INDEX

I

DID YOU BORROW THIS COPY?

Have you been borrowing a copy of *The Responsible Serving of Alcoholic Beverages: A Complete Staff Training Course for Bars, Restaurants, and Caterers* from a friend, colleague, or library? Wouldn't you like your own copy for quick and easy reference? To order, photocopy the form below and send to:

Atlantic Publishing Company
1210 SW 23rd Place • Ocala, FL 34474-7014

Order toll-free 800-814-1132
FAX 352-622-5836

Atlantic Publishing Company
1210 SW 23rd Place • Ocala, FL 34474-7014

Add $5.00 for USPS shipping and handling. For Florida residents PLEASE add the appropriate sales tax for your county.

ALCOHOL SERVICE POSTERS

Decorative and instructional, these full-color posters will be popular with both your employees and customers. Containing essential information, drink photos, recipes, and more, they will help increase sales and grab attention. Posters are laminated to reduce wear and tear and measure 11" x 17".

Series of 7 Posters
Item # ASP-PS • $59.95

12 Classic Cocktails with
Recipes Item # CC-PS • $9.95

12 Popular Cocktails with
Recipes Item # PC-PS • $9.95

Types of Beer
Item # TOB-PS • $9.95

Categories of Liquor
Item # COL-PS • $9.95

10 Types of Martinis
Item # TOM-PS • $9.95

Drink Garnishes
Item # DG-PS • $9.95

Common Bar Abbreviations
Item # CBA-PS • $9.95

WINE SERVICE POSTERS

These five color posters cover all the wine basics—from service to pronunciation. Essential information for anyone serving, pouring, or selling wine, yet attractive enough to display in your dining room. Posters are laminated to reduce wear and tear and measure 11" x 17".

Series of 5 Posters
Item # WPS-PS • $39.95

Wine Pronunciation Guide
Item # WPG-PS • $9.95

Proper Wine Service
Item # PWS-PS • $9.95

Red Wine
Item # RWP-PS • $9.95

White Wine
Item # WWP-PS • $9.95

Sparkling Wine & Champagne
Item # SWC-PS • $9.95

To order call 1-800-814-1132 or visit www.atlantic-pub.com

ALCOHOL AWARENESS POSTER SERIES

Alcohol awareness is an important issue. This new poster series covers ten fundamental topics and should be posted in any establishment that serves alcohol. Posters are in full color and laminated to reduce wear. They measure 11" x 17".

Series of 10 Posters Item # AAP-PS • $89.95

Right to Refuse Service
Item # RTR-PS • $9.95

Drinking & Pregnancy
Item # D&P-PS • $9.95

One Drink Equals
Item # ODE-PS • $9.95

Blood Alcohol Content Chart—
Female Item # BACF-PS • $9.95

Spotting a Fake ID
Item # FID-PS • $9.95

Blood Alcohol Content Chart—Male
Item # BACM-PS • $9.95

Symptoms of Intoxication
Item # SIO-PS • $9.95

Don't Drink & Drive
Item # DDD-PS • $9.95

We Check IDs
Item # CID-PS • $9.95

Alcohol Slows Reaction Times
Item # ASR-PS • $9.95

To order call 1-800-814-1132 or visit www.atlantic-pub.com